OTHER TITLES OF INTEREST FROM ST. LUCIE PRESS

ISO 9000: An Implementation Guide for Small to Mid-Sized Businesses

The 90-Day ISO Manual: Basics Manual and Implementation Guide

Inside ISO 14000: The Competitive Advantage of Environmental Management

Principles of Total Quality

Quality Improvement Handbook: Team Guide to Tools and Techniques

Total Quality Management: Text, Cases, and Readings, 2nd Edition

Introduction to Modern Statistical Quality Control and Management

Focused Quality: Managing for Results

The Executive Guide to Implementing Quality Systems

Total Quality Service: Principles, Practices, and Implementation

For more information about these titles call, fax or write:

St. Lucie Press
100 E. Linton Blvd., Suite 403B
Delray Beach, FL 33483
TEL (407) 274-9906 • FAX (407) 274-9927

S_L^t

QS-9000 HANDBOOK

A GUIDE TO REGISTRATION AND AUDIT

JAYANTA K. BANDYOPADHYAY

S^t_L

St. Lucie Press
Delray Beach, Florida

Phone: (407) 274-9906
Fax: (407) 274-9927

S^t_L

Published by
St. Lucie Press
100 E. Linton Blvd., Suite 403B
Delray Beach, FL 33483

TABLE OF CONTENTS

Appendices

PREFACE

In the coming decade, quality is going to be the entry ticket for any company doing business in the world marketplace. The survival of a business will be at stake unless it can provide high-quality products and/or services. For quite some time, customers have been demanding from their suppliers quality conformance according to specifications, which involves inspection, quality control, and quality assurance auditing. As firms cross frontiers and conduct business all over the world, traditional techniques of inspection, such as receiving and on-site inspection, become costly and nonproductive.

In order to develop a more reliable and cost-effective worldwide interdependent production and distribution system, many nations and their industries have joined in an effort to bring an international series of quality standards known as ISO 9000 to all quality systems, to oversee all production or service operations irrespective of their nature. Instead of inspecting individual products to determine whether they meet required specifications, under ISO 9000 the emphasis is on inspecting the production or service system to make sure that it is sound and is capable of producing products/services of desired quality according to customer requirements.

Although the ISO 9000 quality standards have been welcomed by all industries in general, they are quite generic in nature. The automotive industry has realized that its requirements are much more stringent than the ISO 9000 standards. In June 1988, the purchasing and supply vice presidents of Chrysler Corporation, Ford Motor Company, and General Motors Corporation and the Automotive Division of the American Society for Quality Control chartered a Supplier Quality Requirement Task Force to standardize reference manuals, reporting formats, and technical nomenclature. Previously, each company had its own requirements for supplier quality systems and corresponding assessment documentation. In 1990, the task force created and released *Measurement Systems Analysis (MSA) Manual* and in 1991 developed *Statistical Process Control (SPC) Manual* and *Advanced Product Quality Planning (APQP) Reference Manual and Reporting Format* (available from the Automotive Industry Action Group).

In December 1992, the task force was directed to harmonize the fundamental supplier quality systems manuals and assessment tools. As a result, in August 1994, the task force developed and released *Quality System Requirements: QS-9000*, which is a set of common requirements for all automotive suppliers, based on the ISO 9000 series of quality standards. It includes sector-specific, company-specific, division-specific, and commodity-specific requirements. The task force was confident that when implemented, QS-9000 would improve supplier quality systems by eliminating redundant requirements and reducing the cost of unproductive repetitive inspections.

QS-9000 applies to all internal and external suppliers of raw materials, components, subassemblies, and service parts to Chrysler, Ford, General Motors, a number of heavy truck manufacturers, and their subscribing companies. All requirements of QS-9000 are to be incorporated into the supplier quality systems, described in supplier quality documentation, and verified through third-party registration. General Motors has already mandated that its suppliers must be registered by a third-party quality system registrar no later than December 31, 1997. All Chrysler suppliers must have completed a QS-9000 self-assessment by July 7, 1995 and be registered to QS-9000 by a third-party registrar by July 31, 1997. Ford expects all its suppliers to be registered to QS-9000 by a third-party registrar on or before December 31, 1996. Thus, QS-9000 is having a huge impact on the automotive and truck industry throughout the world. QS-9000 registration is becoming a survival strategy for direct suppliers to the big three automakers and truck manufacturers. Failing to achieve registration to QS-9000 may result in losing competitiveness, or even the business in the long run.

In order to achieve QS-9000 registration, a company must first choose a third-party registrar. Choosing a registrar is critical to deriving benefits from target customers. The registrar must be accredited by an accreditation agency (for example, the RAB, NACCB, and RvC) and recognized by a company's target customers; otherwise, the registration will be of no or little value. In order to achieve registration, a company must provide adequate documentation to prove that it has an effective quality assurance system. Documentation must be simple, clear, and complete, such that on any day any employee can walk into a workstation and be able to perform the job perfectly. A company must also provide substantial evidence that top management is totally committed to continuous quality improvement, including commitment of substantial resources for continuous improvement of the quality system.

A company must also prove that a quality assurance system is in place and working effectively. The quality assurance system under no circumstances is to be placed under the production function, and it should be empowered to prevent the production of inferior products and to assure quality all through the organization. This involves establishing a quality assurance function, reporting directly to top management, which will continuously monitor, control, and assure quality across the organization and document quality activities. For successful implementation of a quality assurance system, it is imperative that a company establish organization-wide quality awareness, an ongoing extensive training program in quality for its employees at all levels and particularly for those who are responsible for quality, and a plan for continuous improvement.

QS-9000 registration is not just a one-time process. Companies that achieve registration are continuously monitored (usually every six months) by their registrars through periodic audits. The registration is valid only for a specific period of time (normally three years), after which a company must apply for reregistration. If a company goes through a reorganization or significant changes in its production or distribution process, it must inform its registrar, and the registrar may reassess the situation.

This book is a practical guide to achieving QS-9000 registration. It can be used by those who want to learn about the QS-9000 quality system requirements and are planning to organize, document, and implement their quality assurance system for QS-9000 registration. The book provides a description and explanation of the QS-9000 quality system requirements and the third-party registration process. It explains how to choose a registrar, how to write documentation, how to plan and carry out internal audits, and how to plan for a third-party audit. It also provides instructions, with examples, for estimating the cost of and time to achieve QS-9000 registration. The appendices include lists of quality system registrars and accrediting bodies, sources of information for the EC market, suggested formats for documentation, a list of acronyms and glossary of terms, and a case study.

The author gratefully acknowledges the support of Richard Hoff and Subir Chowdhury in the preparation of this book.

THE AUTHOR

Jayanta K. Bandyopadhyay, Ph.D., CFPIM, CQA, IQA, QSA, is a tenured Full Professor of Production and Operations Management at Central Michigan University in Mount Pleasant. He earned his B.S. in Mechanical Engineering from Jadavpur University, Calcutta, India in 1961; M.S. in Industrial Engineering and Operations Research from the University of Texas at Austin in 1970; and Ph.D. in Industrial Engineering from Texas Tech University at Lubbock in 1973.

He is certified as a Quality Auditor (CQA) by the American Society for Quality Control, a Provisional International Quality Auditor (IQA) by the Institute of Quality Assurance, a Quality Systems Provisional Auditor (QSA) by the Registrar Accreditation Board of the ASQC, and at the Fellows level in Inventory Management (CFPIM) by the American Production and Inventory Control Society. He is also a member of the Technical Committee for Higher Education of the ASQC.

His research interests include production/operations management, just-in-time production, total quality management, computer-integrated manufacturing, and health care delivery systems planning, design, and control. He has published numerous articles in many professional journals, including *International Journal of Management, Journal of Clinical Engineering, Production and Inventory Management Journal, Interface of the Institute of Management Science,* and *Michigan Academicians.* He is also the author of *Practitioner's Handbook for Implementation and Registration to ISO 9000 Quality Standards* and *CPIM Exam Review with Model Test Questions.*

Dr. Bandyopadhyay was recognized as an Outstanding Teacher in Quantitative Application in Decision Making by Fort Bragg's Extended Learning Program in 1984 and was nominated for an Outstanding Teacher Award at Central Michigan University in 1992, 1993, 1994, and 1995. He was recognized by Central Michigan University as an Outstanding Student Advisor and an Outstanding Thesis Advisor in 1986 and as a Super Professor in 1991 and 1994.

1

INTRODUCTION

In recent years, with the growing volume of international trade, customers have had a wider choice of products and services from around the world. Wider choice elevates quality requirements and poses other new challenges. In a competitive marketplace, high product and service quality alone is not sufficient; success depends upon many other important factors, such as price, variety, speed of delivery, and reliability. In this dynamic and competitive marketplace, companies are under tremendous pressure to become more customer oriented and more cost effective and to continuously improve quality.

Quality and productivity, and in some cases competitiveness, are the key elements of success. Although the basic requirements for successful competition may be well known, many are not widely understood. Few companies have progressed to the point where these requirements have become integrated into their overall management systems. Many are moving through the early stages of quality and productivity management. They promote quality from a narrowly defined quality control function at the lower level but have not yet integrated it with their overall business management systems.

There is a growing consensus that traditional quality control based on inspection is outdated and must be replaced with customer-focused, prevention-based approaches to quality and productivity improvement. The success of this transition is dependent upon many factors, such as top management commitment, worker empowerment, rapid deployment of technology, diversity and innovation, and customer-focused strategy. Thus, competitiveness is a rapidly moving target. To remain competitive, a company must evolve continuously.

The U.S. auto industry has been continuously striving for quality as a means to survive in its own backyard. Toward this end, each of the big three automakers—General Motors, Ford, and Chrysler—has developed numerous standards and specifications which not only confuse many of their suppliers but also place a tremendous burden on them in terms of compliance. It is not uncommon for a supplier to service all of the big three automakers, in which case the supplier has to abide by completely different standards, specifications, and requirements as dictated by each customer. This creates not only confusion but also mountains of documentation and standards, in addition to a profusion of wasteful inspection, testing, and quality assurance activities. While the big three automakers are attempting to cut their costs by maintaining just-in-time inventories, their suppliers must waste their valuable resources to provide just-in-time zero defects quality parts. During the past decade, this situation has severely strained supplier–customer relationships in the automotive industry. In light of all this confusion surrounding quality standards and specifications, all of the big three automakers and some truck manufacturers have finally recognized the need for harmonization and internationalization of their standards, specifications, and requirements.

INTERNATIONAL STANDARDS FOR QUALITY (ISO 9000)

Globalization of the market and tough competition have created a tremendous demand for higher quality and productivity. Companies seeking to serve several different customers face a multitude of separate quality requirements and audits, and traditional methods of quality control, incoming inspection, on-site inspection, etc.

are becoming obsolete, unreliable, and cost ineffective. A critical need thus exists for development of an independent, reliable, consistent, and economical system to assess whether or not a supplier's quality assurance system is in conformance with commonly recognized uniform quality standards. This ultimately led to the International Organization for Standardization's ISO 9000 series of quality standards developed by ISO Technical Committee (TC) 176 in 1987. Many nations approved them instantly, and they became the standards for the world marketplace. This marked a new beginning in Pan-European trade among European Economic Community (EEC) member countries and their trading partners around the world. Each participating country consequently adopted an equivalent version of the ISO 9000 series of quality standards. In 1987, the United States adopted its own version, ANSI/ASQC Q90, using American terminology. The United Kingdom has been using the same standards as BS 5750, while the European countries have adopted the ISO standards as EN 29000.

DEVELOPMENT OF QS-9000 QUALITY SYSTEM REQUIREMENTS

Instead of inspecting an individual product or service to determine if it meets required specifications, the emphasis under ISO 9000 is on auditing the production system or service system to make sure that the system is capable of producing the desired quality of products or services according to customer requirements. While ISO 9000 provides general guidelines for quality system assurance and is applicable to all types of industries, many find it too generic for their particular applications. The big three automakers had already created mountains of standards, policies, and procedures so individualized and cumbersome that they started to choke their suppliers with paperwork and unproductive time devoted to repetitive inspections and audits. They finally realized that they would gain substantial advantages by adopting common standards for all of their supplier bases. In June 1988, representatives from the three automotive original equipment manufacturers (OEMs) and the Automotive Division of the American Society for Quality Control (ASQC) created the Supplier Quality Requirements Task Force to develop a common understanding on topics of mutual interest within the automotive industry.

In 1990, the task force released the *Measurement Systems Analysis: Reference Manual (MSA)*, which is now available through the Automotive Industry Action Group (AIAG). This document provides a common approach for all automotive suppliers to calibrate measurement equipment and evaluate the presence of error in such devices. In 1991, the *Statistical Process Control Reference Manual* was released through the AIAG. This manual provides a common approach to statistical process control in the automotive industry. It was followed by the *Advanced Product Quality Planning (APQP) Reference Manual and Reporting Format*. This manual provides guidelines for preparing plans and checklists to ensure that advanced product quality planning has actually been carried out by the supplier. Finally, in December 1992, the task force was directed to harmonize the fundamental supplier quality system manuals and assessment tools. As a result, in August 1994, the task force developed and released *Quality System Requirements: QS-9000*, which is a common sets of requirements for all automotive suppliers. By September 1994, it was announced that QS-9000 would immediately replace all previous automotive supplier quality programs. A number of heavy truck manufacturers (for example, Mack Trucks, Navistar International, Peterbilt Trucks, Volvo GM Heavy Trucks, Kenworth Trucks, and Freightliner Corporation) also adopted QS-9000. In the future, it is anticipated that most automotive OEMs and their suppliers will adopt QS-9000.

QS-9000 QUALITY SYSTEM REQUIREMENTS

QS-9000 defines the fundamental quality system requirements of the big three automakers (General Motors, Ford, and Chrysler), truck manufacturers, and other subscribing companies. The requirements apply to all internal and external suppliers of raw materials, components, subassemblies, and service parts. QS-9000 is the outcome of the internationalization of quality standards and the harmonization of quality requirements of auto and truck manufacturers. Internationalization involves adoption of ISO 9001:1994 Section 4 as the core quality requirements, while harmonization is the result of blending the existing quality requirements of Chrysler's *Supplier Quality Assurance Manual*, Ford's *Q-101 Quality System Standard*, and General Motors' *NAO Targets for Excellence*, as well as input from truck manufacturers and other subscribing companies. ISO 9002, instead of ISO 9001, forms the core requirements for those suppliers that do not design their products but rather manufacture them from designs specified by their customers. Companies that provide testing and inspection services, such as testing laboratories, use ISO 9003 instead of ISO 9001 or ISO 9002 as core requirements.

QS-9000 aims to provide a common basis for prevention of defects, reduction of variation, elimination of waste, and continuous improvement of quality. It will also serve to develop a common understanding of topics of mutual interest, as well as closer working relationships and better cooperation among all participants within the automotive and truck industry.

ARCHITECTURE OF QS-9000

QS-9000 quality system requirements consist of three distinct sections.

Section I. Core Requirements—This section includes all twenty elements of ISO 9001:1994 Section 4. Each element is exactly the same as provided in the original ISO 9001 document but is in italic type. However, additional requirements as needed for the automotive and trucking industry are described in regular type following each ISO element. Thus, this section may be considered to be an elaboration of each element of ISO 9001:1994 Section 4 specially fit to the needs of the automotive and truck industry.

Section II. Sector-Specific Requirements—This section includes additional requirements beyond the scope of ISO 9001:1994 Section 4 but common to the automotive and truck industry. These requirements include *Production Part Approval Process, Continuous*

Improvement, and *Manufacturing Capabilities*. These programs are already in place within the automotive and truck industry.

Section III. Customer-Specific Requirements—This section includes the unique specific requirements for each individual customer, such as General Motor, Ford, and Chrysler, and truck manufacturers, such as Mack Trucks, Navistar International, Freightliner, Volvo GM Heavy Trucks, and Peterbilt Trucks. Each supplier must also discuss with its customer the unique specific requirements applicable to any existing or future contracts.

QS-9000 REGISTRATION

Conformance to QS-9000 quality system requirements is generally verified by third-party audit by a customer-approved QS-9000 registrar. On rare occasions, a second-party audit by the customer's auditor is allowed. It should be noted that many existing requirements of automakers such as statistical process control (SPC), advanced product quality planning (APQP), failure mode and effects analysis (FMEA), etc. and program requirements such as Chrysler's *Supplier Quality Assurance*, General Motors' *NAO Targets for Excellence*, Ford's *Q-101 Quality System Standard*, and others still prevail under QS-9000 requirements. What have been added are the requirements of ISO 9001 or ISO 9002 and that of a third-party audit. The ISO 9001- or ISO 9002-based requirements and the sector-specific requirements are normally examined by a third-party audit during the registration process, while the customer-specific requirements are usually audited by the customer through a second-party audit. The guidelines for such audits as developed by the Supplier and Quality Requirement Task Force are presented in a document entitled *Quality System Assessment*. This document is also available from the Automotive Industry Action Group.

QS-9000 THIRD-PARTY REGISTRARS

QS-9000 third-party registrars are independent companies that are accredited by a national accreditation body to verify compliance with QS-9000 quality system requirements through a third-party independent audit. They maintain a register of names of companies that have achieved QS-9000 registration through them. The accreditation body for a registrar is either chartered or appointed by the government of the country in which it is located. For example, in the United Kingdom, a registrar must be accredited by the National Accreditation Council for Certification Bodies (NACCB), which issues a certificate with the Crown Stamp of the NACCB. The accreditation body in The Netherlands is Raad voor de Certificatie (RvC). Similarly, most European countries have their own accreditation bodies. In December 1991, the American National Standards Institute (ANSI) and American Society for Quality Control jointly set up the Registration Accreditation Board (RAB) to accredit American registrars of quality systems according to the European Norm (EN) 45000 series of standards, which governs all conformity assessment activities. When choosing a registrar, it is also important to find out whether its certificate will be recognized by your customers.

QS-9000 REGISTRATION MANDATES

General Motors Corporation has already mandated that its suppliers must be registered by a third-party quality system registrar no later than December 31, 1997 (Martin, 1994). For all new suppliers, General Motors has initiated a Potential Supplier Audit by January 1, 1995 based on a Quality Systems Assessment (QSA) document. As of January 1, 1996, General Motors requires third-party registration to the QS-9000 quality system requirements for all new suppliers.

Ford expects all its suppliers to be registered by a third-party registrar to QS-9000 quality system requirements on or before December 31, 1996. Ford has announced that it will perform second-party assessment on an exception basis. Chrysler Corporation has laid down a demanding schedule for QS-9000 implementation by its suppliers. All of Chrysler's suppliers must complete a self-assessment to QS-9000 by July 7, 1995, and all production and service part suppliers to Chrysler must register to QS-9000 by a third-party registrar by July 31, 1997.

WHO SHOULD REGISTER TO QS-9000?

QS-9000 is having a huge impact on the automotive and truck industry throughout the world. All tier one (direct) suppliers to General Motors, Ford, and Chrysler are required to implement QS-9000 quality system requirements by July 1997. All tier one suppliers to the big three automakers and major truck manufacturers in the United States and abroad will have to eventually implement QS-9000 in their quality systems by becoming registered as part of their long-term survival strategy. QS-9000 registration can also provide a company with a sharp competitive edge. It proves the company's capability as a high-quality supplier and can open up a wealth of business opportunities all over the world. Automakers in Japan and other countries may also require their suppliers to register under ISO 9000 or QS-9000 in the future. While many of their suppliers might already be registered under ISO 9000 or QS-9000, ISO 9000 registration does not meet the QS-9000 quality system requirements.

Companies in other industry groups (e.g., appliance, aerospace, electronics, etc.) need not implement QS-9000 unless they supply the big three automakers and truck manufacturers, which might require them to register under QS-9000. Suppliers of equipment, warehousing, and services to the big three automakers and truck manufacturers should also be developing quality plans which would allow them to be included in a common quality system effort in the future. This does not mean that they should rush into registration to QS-9000 but rather that they should discuss with their customers their specific quality system requirements. Considering all these developments, whether located in the United States or abroad, a company should seriously attempt to achieve QS-9000 registration if it wants to be a supplier to:

1. Any of the big three automakers or major truck manufacturers in the United States

2. Any of the suppliers of any of the big three automakers or major truck manufacturers in the United States

3. Any other company whose customer requires QS-9000 registration

Finally, the requirement of QS-9000 registration is not geographically limited to the United States. Any direct supplier of the big three U.S. automakers and major U.S. truck manufacturers, whether located in the United States or abroad, will have to register under QS-9000 in the near future.

OPPORTUNITY WITH QS-9000 REGISTRATION

By registering to the QS-9000 quality system requirements using a third-party registrar, a company can earn recognition as a quality producer of automotive components and service parts and gain tremendous competitive advantages. One advantage is that a company can increase its business significantly not only within the United States but also in the world marketplace. Automakers and truck manufacturers all over the world may become its potential customers. On the other hand, failure to achieve registration may result in loss of business from the big three automakers and truck manufacturers in the United States and possibly from other overseas auto and truck manufacturers.

Once implemented, QS-9000 may save substantial resources previously devoted to repetitive inspection and quality control. Once the system is under control, it is likely to produce good quality products at substantial cost savings. QS-9000 registration also reinforces the customer–supplier relationship as a team concept and can strengthen long-term business relationships, profit potential, growth, and prosperity.

CONCLUSION

The mandate of registration dictated by General Motors, Ford, and Chrysler has placed tremendous pressure upon their supplier bases. There are simply not enough trained and qualified registrars, auditors, and quality personnel to accomplish this monumental task. The laws of supply and demand will dictate the costs and waiting times for a company to become registered to QS-9000. Many suppliers still question the need for third-party registration, debate whether or not to commit the necessary resources to obtain it, and doubt whether it will be cost effective. Because of the mandates by the big three automakers, their suppliers must ask their customers when and how to get started. Each supplier must choose the registrar that fits with its culture, is eager to help the company succeed, has experience in the area of its operations and products, has an unbiased attitude toward the company, and is well recognized by its customers. Finally, implementation of QS-9000 demands total commitment to quality by the supplier's top management. Without this commitment, all efforts will be useless.

2

OVERVIEW OF QS-9000 QUALITY SYSTEM REQUIREMENTS*

The big three automakers—General Motors, Ford, and Chrysler— and major truck manufacturers like Mack Trucks, Navistar International, Peterbilt Trucks, Volvo GM Heavy Trucks, Kenworth Trucks, and Freightliner Corporation have established QS-9000 quality system requirements for all their internal and external suppliers of raw materials, components, subassemblies, and service parts. QS-9000 is the result of the internationalization of quality standards and the harmonization of quality requirements from the big three automakers and truck manufacturers. The international-

---

* This chapter provides an overview and explanation of the QS-9000 standards and requirements as presented in the original document entitled *Quality System Requirements: QS-9000,* published by the Automotive Industry Action Group (AIAG), Southfield, Michigan, which holds the 1994 copyright. No part of this chapter should be considered as the presentation of the original standards, but rather the chapter presents an overview and interpretation of those standards and requirements. For exact and detailed information about the standards and requirements, the original document should be obtained from the AIAG.

11

ization involves adoption of ISO 9001:1994 Section 4 as the core quality requirements, whereas the harmonization blends their existing quality system requirements, for example Chrysler's *Supplier Quality Assurance Manual*, Ford's *Q-101 Quality System Standard*, General Motors' *NAO Targets for Excellence*, and input from truck manufacturers and other subscribing companies. For those suppliers that do not design their own products, ISO 9002 instead of ISO 9001 will form their core quality requirements. Similarly, companies that offer only testing and inspection services, such as testing laboratories, will use ISO 9003 instead of ISO 9001 for their core quality requirements. QS-9000 and other manuals and procedures such as *Advanced Product Quality Planning and Control Plan (APQP)*, *Measurement Systems Analysis (MSA)*, *Statistical Process Control (SPC)*, and *Failure Mode and Effects Analysis (FMEA)* are distributed through the Automotive Industry Action Group.

Quality System Requirements: QS-9000 is comprised of three distinct sections—Section I: ISO 9000 Based Requirements, Section II: Sector-Specific Requirements, and Section III: Customer-Specific Requirements. Also included in the appendix are The Quality System Assessment Process, Code of Practice, Specific Characteristics and Symbols, Local Equivalents for ISO 9001 and 9002 Specifications, Acronyms and Their Meanings, and a Glossary of Terms.

SECTION I: ISO 9000 BASED REQUIREMENTS

ISO 9000 Based Requirements contains the core quality requirements of QS-9000. It includes all twenty elements of the ISO 9001 quality standards. Each element of ISO 9001 is printed verbatim but appears in italic type. Following each element, a description of additional automaker/truck manufacturer requirements as applied to that particular element is provided. Thus, this section can be described as an expansion of ISO 9001:1994 as applied to the automotive/truck industry.

The ISO 9001/Q91 standard is the most comprehensive of all three models for quality assurance systems. It consists of twenty paragraphs, some of which are broken down into a number of subparagraphs, as shown in Table 2.1. The primary scope of the ISO 9001 standard is to ensure that a supplier can demonstrate

TABLE 2.1   ISO 9001/ANSI/ASQC Q91 Subparagraphs

4.1 Management Responsibility
  4.1.1 Quality Policy
  4.1.2 Organization
    4.1.2.1 Responsibility and Authority
    4.1.2.2 Verification Resources and Personnel
    4.1.2.3 Management Representative
  4.1.3 Management Review
  4.1.4 Business Plan
  4.1.5 Analysis and Use of Company-Level Data
  4.1.6 Customer Satisfaction
4.2 Quality System
  4.2.1 General
  4.2.2 Quality System Procedures
  4.2.3 Quality Planning
4.3 Contract Review
4.4 Design Control
  4.4.1 General
  4.4.2 Design and Development Planning
  4.4.3 Organizational and Technical Interfaces
  4.4.4 Design Input
  4.4.5 Design Output
  4.4.6 Design Review
  4.4.7 Design Verification
  4.4.8 Design Validation
  4.4.9 Design Changes
4.5 Document and Data Control
  4.5.1 General
  4.5.2 Document and Data Approval and Issue
  4.5.3 Document and Data Changes
4.6 Purchasing
  4.6.1 General
  4.6.2 Evaluation of Subcontractors
  4.6.3 Purchasing Data
  4.6.4 Verification of Purchased Product
4.7 Control of Customer-Supplied Product
4.8 Product Identification and Traceability
4.9 Process Control
  4.9.1 Process Monitoring and Operator Instructions
  4.9.2 Preliminary Process Capability Requirements
  4.9.3 Ongoing Process Performance Requirements

TABLE 2.1 (continued)   ISO 9001/ANSI/ASQC Q91 Subparagraphs

4.9.4   Modified Preliminary or Ongoing Capability Requirements
4.9.5   Verification of Job Set-Ups
4.9.6   Process Changes
4.9.7   Appearance Items
4.10   Inspection and Testing
4.10.1   General
4.10.2   Receiving Inspection and Testing
4.10.3   In-Process Inspection and Testing
4.10.4   Final Inspection and Testing
4.10.5   Inspection and Test Records
4.11   Control of Inspection, Measuring, and Test Equipment
4.11.1   General
4.11.2   Control Procedure
4.11.3   Inspection, Measuring, and Test Equipment Records
4.11.4   Measurement Systems Analysis
4.12   Inspection and Test Status
4.13   Control of Nonconforming Product
4.13.1   General
4.13.2   Review and Disposition of Nonconforming Product
4.13.3   Control of Reworked Product
4.13.4   Engineering-Approved Product Authorization
4.14   Corrective and Preventive Action
4.14.1   General
4.14.2   Corrective Action
4.14.3   Preventive Action
4.15   Handling, Storage, Packaging, Preservation, and Delivery
4.15.1   General
4.15.2   Handling
4.15.3   Storage
4.15.4   Packaging
4.15.5   Preservation
4.15.6   Delivery
4.16   Control of Quality Records
4.17   Internal Quality Audits
4.18   Training
4.19   Servicing
4.20   Statistical Techniques
4.20.1   Identification of Need
4.20.2   Procedures

that its quality assurance system is organized in such a way that it can prevent the occurrence of nonconformity across all stages, from design to servicing.

Three special terms are consistently used in the ISO 9001, 9002, and 9003 standards:

Supplier Refers to the company preparing for implementation or registration.

Purchaser or Customer Refers to the company receiving the products or services of the supplier. The purchaser determines the quality requirements as a part of the contractual agreement which the supplier's quality assurance system must meet.

Subcontractor Refers to the provider of any purchased products such as raw materials, components, subassemblies, utilities, etc. or any service such as maintenance, transportation distribution, warehousing, etc. to the *supplier*. Examples of subcontractors include distributors, contract warehouses, packagers, laboratories, and instrument calibrators. A subcontractor can be *internal* or *external*. An operation of the supplier is considered as an *internal* subcontractor only if that particular operation is not a part of the supplier's quality assurance system as defined by the supplier.

Unlike other standards which refer to the organization supplying a product or service (i.e., your organization) as either the *manufacturer* (Good Manufacturing Practices, GMP) or the *company* (MIL-Q-9858A and MIL-I-45208A, Malcolm Baldrige Quality Award, and others), the ISO 9001 to 9003 series refers to your company as the *supplier*. Your suppliers are referred to as *subcontractors* and your customers are called *purchasers*.

The ISO 9001/Q91 standard is applicable in contractual situations when a supplier must demonstrate its capability to design, develop, produce, install, and service a product or service. Generally, a supplier's ability to conform to the ISO 9001 standard is assessed via the standard's *Quality System Requirements,* which is a set of twenty paragraphs, each designed to address a specific portion of a quality system as follows.

4.1 Management Responsibility

This paragraph consists of the three original ISO 9000 4.1 subparagraphs plus three additional subparagraphs for industry requirements, for a total of six subparagraphs, each of which highlights a particular top management activity. This paragraph emphasizes that top management is always responsible for quality and must organize and plan for it. Top management cannot delegate its quality responsibility to lower levels of management. Just being involved is not enough; top management must be dedicated and committed to quality and prove it through words, deeds, commitment of resources, consistency, and continuous improvement.

Section 4.1.1 Quality Policy—This subparagraph ensures that the supplier's senior management develops and documents a written quality policy. The supplier's quality policy shall contain its mission, objectives, and guidelines in order to demonstrate the supplier's commitment to quality. This subparagraph also requires the supplier to ensure that its policy is understood, implemented, and maintained at all levels of the organization. It is not enough to say, for example, "This is our policy." The policy must be properly defined and documented. This is one way to disseminate understanding of the quality system through each level of the organization and make sure that the system has been developed, installed, and is being successfully maintained at each level. The goal, mission, and objectives of the system should lead to continuous improvement of company performance in terms of quality, reliability, delivery speed, etc. There are no additional industry requirements for this subsection in QS-9000.

4.1.2 Organization—This subparagraph requires the supplier to define the responsibility and authority (Section 4.1.2.1) of the personnel whose work affects the quality of its products, identify allocation of resources (Section 4.1.2.2) for management performance and verification activities, and designate a management representative (Section 4.1.2.3) who will be solely responsible and authorized to develop and implement the company's quality system.

Section 4.1.2.1 Responsibility and Authority—This subparagraph requires the supplier to clearly define the responsibility, authority, and interrelationship of all personnel whose work affects quality. Often a quality organization chart is used for this purpose. Because the focus is on who has the responsibility and authority to control nonconforming products or services, the supplier must define each position (not necessarily by name) in the organization chart for those function(s) which: (1) initiate action to prevent the occurrence of nonconformity, (2) keep records of all identified quality problems, (3) ensure that solutions or corrective actions are implemented, and (4) monitor the processing, delivery, or installation of nonconforming product until corrective action has been taken. This definition of authority and responsibility should be traceable to top management. To outsiders, the organization must be clearly defined; to insiders, it must be clear exactly what constitutes each individual's responsibilities and authority. Relationships among quality personnel and their relationship to senior management should also be defined. There should be no conflicting or overlapping responsibilities and authority. There are no additional industry requirements for this subsection in QS-9000.

Section 4.1.2.2 Verification Resources and Personnel—This subparagraph requires the supplier to ensure that verification activities such as inspection, testing, design verification, process monitoring, etc. are performed by trained personnel and, most importantly, that these activities are carried out by personnel independent of those who have direct responsibility for the work being performed. This ensures that manufacturing functions, for example, are not given responsibility for inspecting their own work. There are no additional industry requirements for this subsection in QS-9000.

Section 4.1.2.3 Management Representative—This subparagraph requires the supplier to appoint someone as a management representative who shall have the responsibility and authority to ensure that requirements specified in ISO 9001, 9002, or 9003 are implemented and maintained. This person must have a direct link to top management. Often, the quality manager serves as the management representative., but top management may choose to appoint a QS-9000 facilitator or coordinator as the management representative. This could be a full-time or part-time position. The responsibilities of the management representative cover a wide range of diverse activities, such as quality planning, statistical process control, inspection, supplier certification, internal auditing, corrective action, training quality personnel, selecting consultants, customer complaint analysis, liaison with external parties on matters related to the supplier's quality system, and so on.

Additional industry requirements include an *Advanced Product Quality Planning and Control Plan (APQP)* which deals with organizational interfaces. This requires the supplier to have systems in place to manage all activities involved in new product development, prototype building, and production of new products to ensure the quality of new products. It also requires that a multidisciplinary approach be taken in decision making and that the supplier be capable of communicating data and information in formats prescribed by the customer. Typical functions in which these requirements are mandatory include (as provided in the note) engineering/technical, manufacturing/production, industrial engineering, quality/reliability, cost estimating, tooling engineering, maintenance, purchasing, materials management, packaging, servicing products, sales and marketing, management information systems, and subcontracting as necessary.

Section 4.1.3 Management Review—This subparagraph addresses timely review of the quality system. Once the supplier quality system is installed, it is to be reviewed at appropriate intervals by the supplier's senior management to ensure its continued suitability and effectiveness. This review may be formal or informal as long as critical information is reviewed and documented. Activities typically include internal audit, corrective actions, systems monitoring, and any change in regular activities. There are no additional industry requirements for this subsection in QS-9000.

Section 4.1.4 Business Plan—This subparagraph is an additional industry requirement of QS-9000. Although not auditable by a third-party registrar, it most likely may be required by the customer. This subparagraph requires that a comprehensive, formal, and documented business plan be developed by the supplier. Both short-term (one to two years) and long-term (three or more years) plans should be developed. Competitive product analysis and benchmarking inside and outside the supplier's commodity and the automotive industry should be carried out as the basis for preparing the business plan. Current and future expectations of the customer must be determined using a valid process. The plan shall be documented, reviewed, updated, and revised as necessary and communicated throughout the organization as deemed appropriate. A business plan typically includes growth projections, sales projections, market analysis, R&D projections, new product plans, plant/facility plans, financial plans and cost analysis, health and safety plans, environmental plans, customer satisfaction plans, human resource plans, quality and operational performance plans, etc.

The purpose of this requirement is to encourage strategic business planning. Business plans are considered to be proprietary material. They do not have to be reviewed with individual customers and copies do not have to be provided to customers, particularly those customers whose divisions are in direct competition with the supplier.

Section 4.1.5 Analysis and Use of Company-Level Data—This subparagraph is an additional industry requirement. It requires the supplier to maintain records related to quality, productivity, efficiency, effectiveness, and current quality levels for its key products and services. These records should be presented in trend format to determine progress toward achieving goals and for comparison with competitors and/or appropriate benchmarks.

Section 4.1.6 Customer Satisfaction—This subparagraph is an additional industry requirement. It requires the supplier to have a documented process to determine customer satisfaction. This process must be objective and valid to determine trends in customer satisfaction. Some of the commonly used methods are benchmarking, focus groups, surveys, quality function deployment, and audits. The purpose of determining trends is for comparisons with competitors and/or appropriate benchmarks. Customer satisfaction trends shall also be reviewed by top management.

4.2 Quality System

This section includes one original ISO 9000 subparagraph and two additional subparagraphs for industry requirements, for a total of three subparagraphs.

Section 4.2.1 General—This is the original ISO 9000 paragraph which indicates that the supplier shall establish and maintain an effective documented quality system which ensures that the product/service conforms to specified requirements. The formal quality system documentation shall consist of a *quality manual* which shall make reference to *quality system procedures* and outline the structure of the documentation process. Guidance for preparing a quality manual is provided in ISO 10013. The quality manual should address all the requirements in the ISO 9001 standard and any other standards related to the quality system as appropriate for the industry and the supplier. In practice, a quality manual has become a mandatory requirement for QS-9000 registration.

Section 4.2.2 Quality System Procedures—This subparagraph is an additional industry requirement. It requires the supplier to prepare documentation of procedures in accordance with ISO 9001 and the supplier's quality policy as stated in its quality manual. Typical procedures are those related to (1) specifications for raw materials, processes, products, packaging, labeling, etc.; (2) safety systems; (3) purchaser service practices including order entry, product delivery, and billing practices; and (4) purchaser relation practices including policies for sharing information, determining purchaser needs, and analyzing and resolving purchaser complaints. In addition, effective implementation of the quality system must be demonstrated by (1) internal audit reports, (2) quality measures of performance, (3) management review of the quality system, and (4) maintaining quality records. Quality procedures may refer to *work instructions,* which explain how an activity can be successfully performed.

Section 4.2.3 Quality Planning—This subparagraph is an additional industry requirement. It requires that the supplier document how it is planning to meet the specific quality requirements for its products, projects, or contracts. It also requires the supplier to use the *Advanced Product Quality Planning and Control Plan (APQP): Reference Manual* in preparing its quality plan. The manual provides a structured but systematic procedure for developing a quality plan which will support the development of products or services to the satisfaction of the big three automakers and truck manufacturers. It uses a product quality planning cycle approach to identify opportunities for improvement in product design, process design, preproduction, and production stages of the product cycle in pursuit of customer satisfaction and continuous improvement. The manual is available from the Automotive Industry Action Group.

Cross-Functional Teams

While preparing advanced product quality planning (APQP), and especially failure mode and effects analysis (FMEA) and control plans, a team approach to planning must be used to designate *special characteristics.* Cross-functional teams are composed of representatives from the supplier's design, process engineering, production, quality, and other areas; the customer's purchasing, product engineering, quality, and plant personnel; and representatives from subcontractors. These teams should develop and review FMEAs and control plans and finalize special characteristics. They should also develop action plans to reduce the high-risk potential failure modes. The purpose of using cross-functional teams is to promote creative thinking, brainstorming, and synergy in the decision-making process.

Special Characteristics

A unique symbol should be assigned to each special characteristic that affects the safety of products, compliance with government regulations, fit/function, etc. Special characteristics are the result of advanced product quality planning activities that incorporate the "voice of the customer." Appendix C of *Quality System Requirements: QS-9000* provides examples of some special symbols such as the shield, the diamond, and the pentagon, among others.

Feasibility Reviews

Prior to contracting to manufacture any product, the supplier should prepare a feasibility study to determine whether it is capable of producing the product so that it conforms to all engineering requirements and specified volumes of production. Typical approaches used in a feasibility study are design review and a capability study. All feasibility studies must be documented using Section 2.13 Team Feasibility Commitment of the *APQP Reference Manual*.

Process Failure Mode and Effects Analysis

Process failure mode and effects analysis (FMEA) is a systematic review and analysis of any new or revised process to monitor and resolve any potential problems. Emphasis should be on defect prevention rather than defect detection. All process FMEAs should consider all special characteristics of new parts and ensure that all possible improvements to the process have been incorporated before any production starts. Some customers require FMEA review and approval prior to any production part approval. All FMEAs should be documented, reviewed, and updated as new failures are discovered.

Control Plan

A control plan is the outcome of the advanced product quality planning process beyond the development of robust processes. For mature existing products, control plans may be developed based upon existing plans. For new products and new processes, new control plans must be developed. If a current product or process changes or becomes unacceptable or statistically unstable, a new control plan must be developed. Thus, the control plan is a living document.

The control plan must cover the prototype building, prelaunch production, and full production stages. For the prototype building and prelaunch production stages, the control plan must include a description of dimensional measurements, materials used, and performance tests to be performed. For the full production stage, the control plan shall provide comprehensive documentation of product and process characteristics, process control parameters, test requirements, and measurement systems used during the production stage. It is important that the supplier use a cross-functional team in developing the control plan, which shall be approved by the appropriate customer engineering and quality personnel. In some cases, the approval requirement may be waived by the customer or the customer may choose to develop a cross-functional team to prepare the control plan.

4.3 Contract Review

The purpose of the contract review section is to make sure that the supplier and the customer have the same understanding of the requirements under the contract, that the supplier has adequate resources to complete the job under the contract, and that all contract review activities are properly documented and recorded. It involves a set of procedures used by the supplier to assure that it understands and is capable of meeting the purchaser's requirements. Basically, four procedural items are required under this section to ensure that: (1) the contractual requirements are adequately defined and documented, (2) the supplier is capable of meeting the customer's requirements, (3) all requirements that differ from the contractual agreement can be resolved, and (4) all records related to the above transactions are preserved. The supplier should also establish procedures for amending the contract and for correctly transferring that information to the appropriate functions within the supplier's organization. All records of contract review must be maintained by the supplier. No additional requirements have been added to this section for QS-9000

4.4 Design Control

This section is applicable only to those suppliers that design their own products. Those suppliers (qualified for ISO 9002) that do not design their own products but manufacture them according to design specifications supplied by their customers need not abide by the requirements of this section. However, suppliers that sub-contract their design work to an independent design house must make sure that the design house is registered under QS-9000 or that all designs are approved by the customer.

4.4.1 General—The purpose of this section is to ensure that the supplier has a thorough understanding of the specific require-ments of the design and established procedures for verifying and controlling the design process so that any problems and errors can be detected at the drawing board stage. The use of flowcharts in developing these procedures is strongly recommended. This sec-tion ensures that the supplier establishes and maintains proce-dures to control and verify the design of the product or the pro-cess under contract in order to ensure that the specified requirements are met.

There are eight subsections (4.4.2 through 4.4.9) under this section. They cover all developmental and design activities when the supplier undertakes a product or process design project under contract.

4.4.2 Design and Development Planning—This subsection re-quires preparation of plans to identify responsibility for each de-sign and developmental activity and describe how these plans will be updated during the development cycle. Qualified staff and ad-equate resources must be assigned to each design activity. In ad-dition, QS-9000 requires that the design staff possess a wide range of design skills such as geometric dimensioning and tolerancing, value engineering, quality function deployment, design of experi-ments, solid modeling, finite element analysis, failure mode and effects analysis, reliability engineering, computer-aided design and engineering, design for manufacturing and assembly, and com-puter simulation as needed for specific design activities normally carried out in the department.

4.4.3 Organizational and Technical Interfaces—This subsec-tion requires identification of organizational and technical inter-faces among the various groups involved. The type of documented information that flows across these various interfaces must be identified and regularly reviewed. It may be helpful to prepare a checklist for design activities to cover items such as composition of the design team and a responsibility matrix to cover customer requirements/statutory requirements and schedule of design reviews/approving authorities.

4.4.4 Design Input—This subsection requires identification and documentation of design input requirements including statutory and regulatory requirements. The supplier shall also identify the personnel who will be responsible for identifying, documenting, verifying, and resolving ambiguous or conflicting input design requirements. In addition, QS-9000 requires that the supplier must have adequate resources to utilize computer-aided design and engineering and that the system is capable of two-way interface with the customer's system. Even if the design is subcontracted, the supplier is still responsible and should provide technical leadership. However, the customer may waive the requirement for a computer-aided system.

4.4.5 Design Output—This subsection requires that procedures be established to document design output requirements and verify how they meet input requirements, conform to regulatory requirements, and meet other safety and functional requirements. It also requires that all design outputs must be reviewed before their release. In addition, QS-9000 requires the supplier to make every effort to simplify, optimize, and reduce waste; use geometric dimensioning and tolerancing as needed; perform value engineering tradeoff analysis and failure mode and effects analysis; and use feedback data from testing, manufacturing, and the field to improve the output from the design process.

4.4.6 Design Review—This subsection requires that formal documented reviews of all designs be planned and carried out at appropriate stages by specialists as well as representatives from all functions concerned. Reviews are critical to the design process as they provide input, verification, and feedback for new idea generation. Competent personnel must be assigned the task of verifying the design. All design review information shall be recorded and maintained.

4.4.7 Design Verification—This subsection requires the verification of designs at each appropriate stage to make sure that design stage output meets the input requirements of the next design stage. All design verification activities and results must be recorded. In addition, QS-9000 requires that a comprehensive prototype development program be developed unless it is waived by the customer or the product is a standardized item. It also requires that the same subcontractors that were used during prototype development be used during the production stage. All products being developed must undergo performance testing for their life, reliability, and durability. All testing activities must be conducted and monitored in a timely fashion to allow timely completion of the project in conformance to customer requirements. All test results shall be recorded. Even if these activities are subcontracted, the supplier must provide technical leadership.

4.4.8 Design Validation—This subsection ensures that the product as designed conforms to the need of the customer or user. Validation is generally performed on a final product under normal operating conditions. In the case of multiple intended uses of a product, multiple validations may be required.

4.4.9 Design Changes—This subsection requires that procedures be established and maintained to identify, document, and periodically review all changes and modifications to the design. It also requires that all design changes be approved by authorized personnel only. In addition, QS-9000 requires that all design changes, even those suggested by subcontractors, be approved in writing by the customer before being implemented, unless this requirement is waived by the customer. For proprietary designs, the customer must be consulted to determine the effects of design changes on form, fit, function, durability, and performance of the product.

4.5 Document and Data Control

4.5.1 General—This section ensures that all documents and data are properly maintained and controlled by the supplier. The requirements are applicable to both internal as well as external documents and data, such as standards and customer drawings.

This section requires that the supplier establish and maintain documented procedures to make available the currently released editions of all documents and data such as standards, customer drawings and specifications, all referenced materials, and other documents deemed necessary by the customer at all appropriate manufacturing locations. For example, engineering drawings and standards, inspection and test procedures, quality manuals, quality procedures, work instructions, etc. must be readily available. It also requires that the supplier use the same symbols or notations for special characteristics as provided in Appendix C of *Quality System Requirements: QS-9000,* published by the Automotive Industry Action Group, or equivalent symbols or notations in consultation with the customer to indicate those process steps which affect special characteristics such as *safety, critical, key, significant,* etc. Documents and data can be maintained as hard copy, in electronic format, or using any other medium. Two subsections (4.5.2 and 4.5.3) further enforce the document control procedures as they relate to the requirements of this standard.

4.5.2 Document and Data Approval and Issue—This subsection requires that procedures be in place to review and approve all documents for adequacy by authorized personnel prior to their issue, to ensure that appropriate documents are available at all locations where operations essential to the effective functioning of the quality system are performed and to ensure that obsolete documents are promptly removed from all locations. All customer source documents must be readily available, whereas customer reference documents may be stored locally.

4.5.3 Document and Data Changes—This subsection requires that procedures be in place to ensure that all document changes and modifications, unless otherwise specified, be performed by the same functions/organizations that performed the original review and approval, that the nature of the changes be identified within the document or the appropriate attachment, and that after a practical number of revisions the document must be reissued.

4.6 Purchasing

This section, which contains four subsections, ensures that products purchased by the supplier conform to specified requirements. In order to do so, (1) the supplier shall select its subcontractors based on their ability to meet subcontract requirements; (2) the selection process and type of quality assurance control used to assess subcontractors shall be based on the type of product as well as history of past performance; (3) records of acceptable subcontractors and some measure of the effectiveness of their quality system need to be considered; (4) the selection of subcontractors and the type and extent of control may depend upon the type of products and the records of the subcontractors' demonstrated performance; (5) purchase documents should contain information that clearly describes (using type, class, style, grade, etc.) the product ordered, the title or other positive identification, applicable specifications, drawings, process requirements, inspection instructions, and other relevant technical information including requirements for approval; and (6) the title, number, and issue of the quality system standard to be applied to the product must be specified.

The last subsection addresses special situations where the purchaser or its representative reserves the right, as per contractual requirements, to verify upon receipt or at source that purchased product conforms to specified requirements. If the customer elects to carry out verification at the supplier's subcontractor's plant, that should not be used by the supplier as evidence of effective control of quality by the subcontractor.

There are a number of additional requirements in this section under QS-9000.

4.6.1 General—This subsection is related to *Approved Materials for Ongoing Production*. It requires that suppliers buy only from a customer-approved list of subcontractors and that any new subcontractor be approved by the customer's materials engineering department.

4.6.2 Evaluation of Subcontractors—This subsection requires the supplier to develop the subcontractor's quality system according to Sections I and II of QS-9000 using quality system assessment at appropriate frequency or that the subcontractor be assessed under QS-9000 by the customer, a customer-approved original equipment manufacturer second-party audit, or an accredited third-party registrar. It also requires the supplier to demand 100% on-time delivery performance of its subcontractor, provide its subcontractor with adequate planning information and purchase commitments so that the subcontractor can plan accordingly, and implement a system to monitor the on-time delivery performance of its subcontractor.

4.6.3 Purchasing Data—This subsection requires that all materials and processes used in part manufacturing must comply with all government, safety, and other regulations and that the supplier comply with and maintain data related to government and safety regulations for restricted and hazardous materials and processes.

4.7 Control of Customer-Supplied Product

This section addresses issues relating to products (e.g., subcomponents) supplied by the customer to the supplier for assembly or incorporation by the supplier into supplies. In such cases, this section requires that the supplier must establish and maintain control procedures, including record keeping, for verification, storage, and maintenance of the customer-supplied product. If any such product is lost, damaged, or cannot be used, it must be recorded and reported to the customer. Despite this verification procedure, the customer remains responsible for providing acceptable products. There are no additional requirements under QS-9000 in this section.

4.8 Product Identification and Traceability

This section requires the supplier to develop and maintain procedures for product identification and traceability during all stages of production, delivery, and installation. Where and to what extent traceability is required and which individual product or batch should be uniquely identified shall be determined and recorded by the supplier. There are no additional requirements in this section under QS-9000.

4.9 Process Control

This section addresses control of production processes and requires the supplier to identify and plan the production and, where applicable, installation processes which directly affect quality and to ensure that these processes are carried out under controlled conditions. This means that the supplier must: (1) document work instructions which relate to production and installation of those processes for which absence of such instructions would adversely affect quality; (2) document work instructions for use of suitable production and installation equipment, suitable working environment, compliance with standards/codes, and quality plans; (3) monitor and control suitable processes and product characteristics during production and/or installation; (4) approve processes and equipment as appropriate; and (5) determine criteria of workmanship which can be stipulated in written standards. For *special processes* whose effectiveness can only be measured after the product is in use, continuous monitoring and/or compliance with documented procedures is required to ensure that their special requirements are met. This section also requires that records be maintained for all qualified processes, equipment, and personnel, as appropriate.

There are several additional requirements in this section under QS-9000. They are related to: (1) *government safety and environmental regulations*—the supplier is required to comply with all environmental and safety regulations in connection with handling, recycling, and disposal of hazardous materials; (2) *designation, documentation, and control of special characteristics as requested by the customer*—the supplier is required to provide documentation showing compliance; and (3) *planned preventive maintenance of key process equipment*—the supplier is required to develop an effective total preventive maintenance system which includes a procedure describing preventive maintenance activities, schedule of maintenance activities, and predictive maintenance methods based upon equipment manufacturers' recommendations. In order to clarify these conditions, several subsections have been added to this section of QS-9000, the primary focus of which is the use of statistical and other methods of process control.

4.9.1 Process Monitoring and Operator Instructions—This subsection requires the supplier to provide at each workstation documented process monitoring and operator instructions to employees who have responsibility for operation of processes. Process sheets, inspection and laboratory test instructions, test procedures, and standard operations sheets are examples of some of these types of operator instructions. This subsection also requires that these instructions include or reference thirteen individual requirements (viz. number and name of the operation, part number and part name, current engineering level date, required tools and gages, relevant engineering and manufacturing standards, customer-designated special characteristics, materials identification and disposition instructions, statistical process control requirements, inspection and testing instructions, corrective action instructions, visual aids if any, set-up instruction and tool change intervals, and revision date and approvals) as listed under this subsection of QS-9000, as appropriate.

4.9.2 Preliminary Process Capability Requirements—This subsection requires that a preliminary process capability study be conducted for all new processes involved with supplier- or customer-designated special characteristics. A preliminary production performance target (Ppk) of 1.67 (if no target is set by the customer) should be achieved within thirty production days. The Ppk results must be reviewed with the customer throughout the various stages of production and quality planning. It also requires that mistake-proof techniques and other QS-9000 Section II techniques be used for continuous process improvement. For planning process improvement activities, attribute data from previous production runs should be used to set priorities.

4.9.3 Ongoing Process Performance Requirements—This subsection addresses cases where the customer may establish some requirements related to performance, use of control plans and charts, and continuous improvement of ongoing production processes. In the absence of any such customer requirements, the supplier should aim to achieve a target Ppk > 1.33 for stable processes and a Cpk > 1.67 for chronically unstable but predictable processes. For nonnormal and unpredictable processes, other methods such as parts per million (ppp), nonparametric analysis, or other index methods may be used to determine performance requirements. All significant events such as tool change, machine repair, etc. should be noted on control charts. This subsection also requires the supplier to initiate an appropriate reaction plan from the control plan to show containment of process outputs and 100% inspection for unstable or noncapable processes. Above all, continuous improvement of processes with higher priority on special characteristics is considered an essential requirement in this subsection.

4.9.4 Modified Preliminary or Ongoing Capability Requirements—This subsection requires that in cases where the customer requirement is higher or lower than the normal or default requirements, the supplier must modify its control plan accordingly.

4.9.5 Verification of Job Set-Ups—This subsection requires that documented instruction be available for all set-ups and that all job set-ups be verified to assure that the parts produced meet all requirements.

4.9.6 Process Changes—This subsection requires that any changes in part number, engineering data, manufacturing process, manufacturing location, material source, and process environment be approved by the customer's production part approval function. Records of all process changes must be maintained.

4.9.7 Appearance Items—This subsection requires that evaluation of customer-designated "appearance items" be performed by qualified persons with appropriate lighting using appropriate masters and evaluation equipment.

4.10 Inspection and Testing

This section contains five subsections which address acceptance criteria and inspection procedures.

4.10.1 General—This subsection requires that the supplier develop and maintain a quality plan or documented procedures for

all inspection and testing activities in order to verify that the product specification requirements have been met. In addition, this subsection of QS-9000 requires that zero defects acceptance criteria be set for all attribute data sampling plans and that accredited laboratories be used for inspection and testing.

4.10.2 Receiving Inspection and Testing—This subsection requires that all incoming parts and materials from subcontractors be inspected or verified before they are used or processed. However, for urgent production purposes, an incoming product may be released without prior inspection, but it must be positively identified and recorded so that it can be immediately recalled and replaced in case of nonconformance to customer requirement. In addition, this subsection of QS-9000 recommends that the supplier's receiving quality system use any one or more of the following techniques to control incoming materials: (1) statistical data, (2) receiving inspection, (3) second- or third-party quality audit of the subcontractor, (4) evaluation by accredited test laboratory, and (5) subcontractor warranty.

4.10.3 In-Process Inspection and Testing—This subsection requires that all inspection and testing be carried out according to the quality plan and documented procedures and that the product be released only after the required inspection and tests have been completed and necessary reports received and verified. However, products may be released under positive-recall procedures outlined in Section 4.10.2 for urgent production purposes. In addition, this subsection of QS-9000 requires that all activities be directed toward error prevention, such as statistical process control, and mistake-proofing rather than error detection and rejection.

4.10.4 Final Inspection and Testing—This subsection requires that all final inspection and testing activities be carried out according to the quality plan and documented procedures and that no product be dispatched until all such activities have been successfully completed and data and documentation have been recorded and authorized. In addition, this subsection of QS-9000 requires the supplier to perform a layout inspection and functional verification for all products at a frequency specified by the customer and that such data be available for review upon request by the customer.

4.10.5 Inspection and Test Records—This subsection requires that all inspection and test results be recorded and maintained for each product. The record should also identify the inspection authority responsible for the release of the product. There are no additional requirements under QS-9000 in this subsection.

4.11 Control of Inspection, Measuring, and Test Equipment

The primary emphasis of this section is on calibration, measurement, accuracy, and precision of inspection, measuring, and test equipment, whether owned by the supplier, on loan, or provided by the customer, to demonstrate conformance of product to specified requirements. This section includes four subsections.

4.11.1 General—This subsection requires that the supplier establish and maintain documented procedures to control, calibrate, and maintain inspection, measuring, and test equipment including software. Such procedures should be used in a manner which ensures that measurement uncertainty is known and is consistent with measurement capability. It also requires that for all of these activities, records of inspections (including frequency of inspection) be kept and instruments be tagged or otherwise identified to indicate the last and the next calibration dates.

4.11.2 Control Procedure—This subsection lists nine control procedures related to selection of appropriate inspection, measuring, and test equipment; calibration procedures; identification of records; maintenance of calibration records; environmental condition; handling; preservation; and safeguard of inspection, measuring, and test equipment and facilities including test hardware and software.

4.11.3 Inspection, Measuring, and Test Equipment Records — This subsection is an additional requirement under QS-9000. It requires that all records of calibration of all inspection, measuring, and test equipment (including those owned by employees) must include all revisions due to engineering changes, conditions and actual readings as received for calibration, and notification to the customer if any suspect product has been shipped.

4.11.4 Measurement Systems Analysis—This is an additional requirement under QS-9000. It requires that appropriate statistical analysis be performed to analyze the variation in the results of each type of inspection, measuring, and test equipment system. This requirement is applicable to all measurement systems referenced in the customer-approved quality control plan. It is also suggested that the *Measurement Systems Analysis* reference manual be used in determining the appropriate acceptance criteria and analytical methods for this purpose.

4.12 Inspection and Test Status

This section requires that throughout production and installation, the inspection and test status of the product be identified using markings, authorized stamps, tags, labels, routing cards, inspection records, test software, physical location, or other suitable means to indicate conformance or nonconformance of products with regard to inspection and test performed. It also requires that the identification of inspection and test status be recorded and maintained, as necessary, throughout the production and installation processes, and that whenever nonconforming product is released, records must be established and maintained in order to identify the inspection authority responsible for its release. In addition, under QS-9000 this section requires that products that fail to pass inspection be placed in a designated area and tagged as rejects to prevent their being returned to the production line by mistake and contaminating other finished products. In cases where the customer requires special *supplemental verification* such as early launch controls, such verification should also be met by the supplier.

4.13 Control of Nonconforming Product

This section emphasizes establishing and maintaining procedures to prevent the inadvertent use or installation of nonconforming product.

4.13.1 General—This subsection requires that all nonconforming product be identified, segregated when practical, documented, and evaluated and that the appropriate functions concerned be notified. This subsection applies to both suspect product and nonconforming product.

4.13.2 Review and Disposition of Nonconforming Product—This subsection addresses the review and disposition of nonconforming product. Under this subsection, the supplier is required to identify who is responsible for the review and disposition (rework, regrade, reject, or accept as is) of nonconforming product. When contractually required, the proposed use of nonconforming or reworked product must be reported to the customer or the customer's representative for concession, and any such concession must be recorded. This subsection also requires that all repaired product be reinspected in accordance with the quality plan or documented procedure and that a description of the nonconformance or repaired or reworked product thus accepted must be recorded and the actual condition noted.

4.13.3 Control of Reworked Product—This subsection is an additional requirement under QS-9000. It requires that all rework instructions be accessible and utilized by appropriate employees in their work areas. It also requires that the supplier establish a prioritized defect reduction plan. At the same time, this subsection prohibits any visible rework on the exterior of any service parts without prior approval of the customer's service parts function.

4.13.4 Engineering-Approved Product Authorization—This subsection is also an additional requirement under QS-9000. It requires the supplier to obtain prior authorization from the customer for any change in product or process. The supplier is also required to maintain a record of such authorization (including expiration date and quantity authorized) by the customer. When shipping materials, authorization needs to be identified on each shipping container. It is suggested that the *Production Part Approval Process* manual be referenced for additional information.

4.14 Corrective and Preventive Action

This section addresses corrective and preventive action activities. It contains three subsections.

4.14.1 General—This subsection requires the development and maintenance of documented procedures for corrective and preventive action. An additional requirement under this subsection of QS-9000 requires that *disciplined problem-solving methods* be used to solve problems related to external or internal noconformities.

4.14.2 Corrective Action—This subsection requires that the supplier's corrective action procedures address: (1) the cause(s) of nonconformity in order to implement effective and lasting corrective actions and prevent recurrence; (2) analysis of all relevant quality records including service reports, customer complaints, work instructions, process controls, and concessions for detecting and eliminating potential causes of nonconforming product; (3) preventive actions to deal with the problem at a level that corresponds to the potential risk; (4) implementation of corrective actions to make sure that they are effective; and (5) recording of necessary procedural changes as a result of such corrective action(s). In addition, this subsection of QS-9000 requires that the supplier analyze parts returned from the customer's facilities and maintain records of analyses, to be made available upon request by the customer.

4.14.3 Preventive Action—This subsection requires that the supplier's preventive action procedures address: (1) use of appropriate sources of information, (2) necessary steps for problem solving and problem prevention, (3) effectiveness of preventive actions, and (4) maintaining preventive action records for management review.

4.15 Handling, Storage, Packaging, Preservation, and Delivery

This section addresses handling, storage, packaging, preservation, and delivery of product by the supplier. It contains six subsections.

4.15.1 General—This subsection requires that the supplier develop and maintain documented procedures for safe handling, storage, packaging, and delivery of products.

4.15.2 Handling—This subsection addresses the safe handling of products.

4.15.3 Storage—This subsection requires the use of designated storage areas and appropriate methods for receipt and dispatch of product from such designated storage areas. It also requires cycle counting of inventory to determine the condition of product in storage areas. The additional requirement in this section under QS-9000 is that the supplier develop and maintain an inventory management system to continuously optimize inventory turnover and inventory levels.

4.15.4 Packaging—This subsection requires the use of appropriate control in packing, packaging, and labeling according to customer requirements. It suggests the use of customer packaging standards and guidelines and the use of an appropriate labeling system according to customer requirements.

4.15.5 Preservation—This subsection requires that the supplier use appropriate preservation and segregation methods while storing materials.

4.15.6 Delivery—This subsection requires that the supplier provide protection of the quality of product after final inspection and, where contractually required, extend this protection until delivery to the customer. An additional requirement of this section of QS-9000 is that the supplier should establish 100% on-time delivery to its customers. It also requires development of a system to improve delivery performance in cases where the 100% on-time delivery goal is not met. The supplier is also required to use a systematic approach to monitor adherence to lead times and to track delivery performance. This subsection also recommends the use of order-driven production scheduling activities and synchronous manufacturing. It requires that the supplier use computerized on-line data transmission for advance shipment notification at the time of shipment and maintain a back-up system in case the on-line system fails.

4.16 Control of Quality Records

This section emphasizes the establishment of procedures for the identification, collection, record keeping, maintenance, retention, storage, availability, and disposition of all quality records, including those of subcontractors, in order to demonstrate achievement of the required quality level and effectiveness of the quality system. This section also requires that all quality records be legible and identifiable to the product involved, easily retrievable, and stored in a suitable environment to prevent damage, deterioration, and loss. Retention times of quality records must be established and recorded. Where contractually agreed, quality records must be made available to the customer's representative for review. Records may be stored using any media, such as paper or in electronic format. Under this section of QS-9000, there are additional requirements related to record retention. All technical records such as tooling records, purchase orders, and parts approvals should be kept as long as the part is active plus one calendar year. All quality performance records such as inspection results, control charts, etc. must be maintained for one calendar year from their creation. Records of internal audits and management review should be kept for three years. This section also requires that copies of documents for superseded parts be kept in the new part file.

4.17 Internal Quality Audits

This section emphasizes the need for internal quality audits. Once a quality system is in place, the supplier shall carry out a comprehensive planned and documented internal audit to ensure that the system is effective and indeed in compliance with said requirements. These audits must be planned and scheduled, and all findings and follow-up actions must be recorded and maintained. The results of the audits shall be brought to the attention of the personnel responsible in the audited area, who in turn shall take timely corrective action on the deficiencies found by the audits. As an additional requirement of QS-9000 under this section, the internal audits should include information on the working environment, as the working environment has a significant effect on product quality.

4.18 Training

Training can be the most costly activity carried out by a supplier. This section requires that the supplier establish and maintain procedures to identify the training needs of all personnel whose work affects quality. For example, internal auditors must be qualified and trained prior to conducting internal audits. Appropriate records of all training should be maintained. Training may go beyond quality-related activities and include safety and technical areas. This section of QS-9000 places tremendous emphasis on training, viewing it as a *strategic issue,* and requires periodic evaluation of the effectiveness of training. Ford Motor Company has developed a program entitled *Ford Instructional Systems Design Process* (by Cvercko, Antonelli, and Steele, 1992) for its own employees and employees of its suppliers.

4.19 Servicing

This section applies only to companies that are contractually obligated to provide servicing activities. Therefore, for some companies, this section may not be applicable. For others, where servicing is an important activity, it merely states that servicing procedures shall meet specified requirements. Defining what the specified requirements are can be a policy decision for companies that do provide servicing. Under QS-9000, this section requires the establishment and maintenance of procedures for feedback of servicing information to all departments involved within the supplier's company.

4.20 Statistical Techniques

This section is often misinterpreted as requiring the supplier to implement statistical process control (SPC) techniques.

4.20.1 Identification of Need—This subsection states that "where appropriate," the supplier shall identify "adequate statistical techniques for verifying the acceptability of process capability and product characteristics." No reference is ever made to SPC or other techniques. Therefore, the supplier may choose the appropriate statistical techniques for inspection, process control, and other activities. In most cases, however, the customer specifies which statistical techniques it would like the supplier to use. Invariably, SPC may be one of those techniques.

4.20.2 Procedures—This subsection requires the establishment and maintenance of documented procedures for the implementation of statistical techniques. As an additional requirement under this subsection of QS-9000, all statistical methods for each process must be chosen during the advanced quality planning stage and included in the quality control plan. Appropriate employees in the supplier's organization are also required to be knowledgeable in basic statistical concepts.

SECTION II: SECTOR-SPECIFIC REQUIREMENTS

Section II covers sector-specific requirements auditable by a third-party registrar. It contains three sections: *Production Part Approval Process, Continuous Improvement,* and *Manufacturing Capabilities.*

1 Production Part Approval Process

This section addresses the production part approval process. It includes two subsections.

1.1 General—This subsection requires that the supplier follow the *Production Part Approval Process* (PPAP) manual in notifying the customer when a new part is designed, major changes are made to the design of an existing part, or changes are made in the production process in terms of location, material, or machinery. This subsection holds the supplier responsible for subcontractor-supplied products and services. It also requires additional approval for parts designated "appearance items" by the customer.

1.2 Engineering Change Validation—This subsection requires the supplier to verify that all changes to products and processes have been properly validated according to the PPAP manual.

2 Continuous Improvement

This section emphasizes the use of the continuous improvement philosophy throughout the supplier's organization. It contains three subsections.

2.1 General—This subsection requires that the supplier continuously improve quality, delivery speed, and price for its customers. For processes important to the customer, the supplier must develop specific action plans for continuous improvement. For variable data, continuous improvement must lead to reduction of variation around the target values for all characteristics and parameters. For attribute data, it means continuous perfection of the process used to make the product. The continuous improvement philosophy should also be extended to all support and business services.

2.2 Quality and Productivity Improvements—This subsection requires the supplier to identify quality and productivity improvement opportunities (such as excessive cycle time, scrap, repair and rework, excessive variation, unscheduled downtime, customer dissatisfaction, etc.) and use appropriate methods to improve them. Documented evidence of improvement should be provided not just in one area but in all areas, including production, engineering, marketing, financial management, human resource management, and facility management.

2.3 Techniques for Continuous Improvement—This subsection requires the supplier to demonstrate knowledge of various improvement techniques such as control charts, Pareto chart, design of experiment, theory of constraints, benchmarking, value engineering, quality vs. cost, etc. and various measures such as parts per million (ppm), capability indices (Cpk), etc.

3 Manufacturing Capabilities

This section addresses issues related to the improvement of manufacturing capabilities. It contains four subsections.

3.1 Facilities, Equipment, Process Planning, and Effectiveness— This subsection requires the use of cross-functional teams in developing plans for manufacturing facilities, production processes, and equipment; use of synchronous manufacturing and value-added use of floor space in plant layout; and due consideration to overall work plan, line balance, automation, ergonomics, human factors, inventory buffer, and value-added labor in developing methods for evaluating the effectiveness of existing processes and operations. The purpose is to identify opportunities for the continuous improvement of manufacturing capabilities.

3.2 Mistake-Proofing—This subsection requires the use of a mistake-proof or *poka yoke* system in the planning of all production processes, manufacturing facilities, toolings, and equipment in order to prevent production of nonconforming products. The use of mistake-proof methods applies to all situations, including existing or potential problems.

3.3 Tool Design and Fabrication—This subsection assigns full responsibility to the supplier for the design, fabrication, and inspection of all toolings and gages, even if they are subcontracted. It also requires that all tools, gages, and equipment owned by the customer be permanently marked and visible.

3.4 Tooling Management—This subsection requires the supplier to develop and maintain an appropriate system to manage tools, gages, and equipment, including machine set-up, tool change, storage, retrieval, and maintenance and repair of facilities. It also holds the supplier responsible for all the above-mentioned works even if they are subcontracted, in which case the supplier is required to develop a tracking and follow-up system.

SECTION III: CUSTOMER-SPECIFIC REQUIREMENTS

The requirements under Section III are not auditable by a third-party registrar, but can be included in a second-party audit by the customer. These requirements address those areas where harmonization was not possible and each individual company therefore maintains its special characteristics in order to gain a competitive advantage in its own unique way. A number of reference manuals are mentioned in this section, and suppliers are expected to acquire copies of each manual and make them available to their employees. This is auditable by a third-party auditor under Section 4.5 Document and Data Control.

Chrysler-Specific Requirements

The nine elements under this section are required by Chrysler Corporation.

Parts Identified with Symbols

Chrysler Corporation uses three special symbols in its designs and blueprints to control the manufacturing process: the *shield*, the *diamond*, and the *pentagon*. Each symbol has specific requirements.

The Shield (S)—Any raw material, component, subassembly, or assembly identified with the shield is required to have special manufacturing control to assure compliance with government vehicle safety requirements and any special requirements as specified in *Shields—Critical Characteristics Guidelines*, published by Chrysler Corporation.

The Diamond (D)—Any raw material, component, subassembly, or assembly identified by the diamond is critical to the function of the part and in particular its quality, reliability, and durability as specified in *Diamond—Critical Characteristics Guidelines*, published by Chrysler Corporation. The diamond represents critical requirements to assure against functional failure. Whereas the shield represents regulatory requirements, the diamond identifies critical functional requirements. The presence of a diamond does not therefore affect the significance of a shield on the same document.

The Pentagon (P)—This symbol identifies special characteristics for initial product parts, developmental parts, toolings, gages, and fixtures as detailed in *Pentagon—Critical Verification Symbol Guidelines*, published by Chrysler Corporation.

Significant Characteristics

These are special characteristics assigned by the supplier based upon knowledge of the product and the production process. They must be included in the supplier's quality control plan.

Annual Layout

This element requires that a complete annual layout inspection of the supplier be made unless written permission is given by the appropriate representative of Chrysler Corporation.

Internal Quality Audits

This element requires that the supplier conduct at least once a year an audit of its internal quality audit system, unless an exception is granted by the appropriate representative of Chrysler Corporation. This audit does not necessarily have to be a third-party audit, but it must be conducted by an independent auditor chosen by the supplier that does not have any vested interest in the area of audit. All such audit records must be preserved.

Design Validation/Production Verification

This element requires that design validation and production verification must be performed on all new and carryover products at least once per model year, unless otherwise specified by the customer.

Corrective Action Plan

This element requires that all Chrysler Corporation suppliers submit a written corrective action plan according to the format specified in *Chrysler 7D Manual* to address all nonconformances. All corrective action plans must be documented and include a description of the problem, cause of the problem, interim action taken including dates, permanent action with effective dates, verification of corrective actions, and control and prevention methods.

Packaging, Shipping, and Labeling

This element requires that all packaging, shipping, and labeling by the supplier must conform with instructions provided in *Packaging and Shipping Instructions Manual* and *Shipping/Parts Identification Label Standards Manual*, published by Chrysler Corporation.

Process Sign-Off

Chrysler Corporation requires its suppliers to perform a systematic and sequential review of their processes. Advanced quality planning teams are required to perform process sign-offs on new products in order to determine the readiness of the process and level of understanding of program requirements.

Chrysler Bibliography

Seven reference manuals are published by Chrysler Corporation. They are generally referred to as the *Blue Dot Series*. These manuals provide valuable information and are available to all Chrysler suppliers. The seven manuals are

1. *Design Review Guidelines*
2. *Design Verification Plan & Report*
3. *Reliability Functions*
4. *Reliability Testing*
5. *Test Sample Planning*
6. *Priority Parts Quality Review*
7. *Product Assurance Guidelines*

Ford-Specific Requirements

The fourteen elements under this section are required by Ford Motor Company.

Control Item (∇) Parts

Control item parts are critical parts that affect the safe operation of a vehicle or compliance with government regulations. They are identified by Ford product engineering with an inverted delta (∇) preceding the part number. The following are the special requirements for all control item parts.

Control Plans and Failure Mode and Effects Analysis (FMEA)— Ford Motor Company requires that control plans and FMEAs for all control item parts be approved by its design and quality engineering function. Any revision to these documents also needs the same approval. These are considered *living documents* which must be maintained on the shop floor and be available to workers. In cases where the supplier is responsible for design, a design FMEA must also be prepared and approved.

Shipping Container Label—Shipping labels for control item parts must contain the inverted delta in front of all Ford part numbers according to the *Packaging Guidelines for Production Parts*, Form 1750 for North America and 1750 EU for Europe, published by Ford Motor Company.

Equipment Standard Parts—The U.S. federal government and Canadian government have designated certain control parts such as seat belts, tires, brake hoses, glazing materials, etc. as *equipment standard parts* and subject to safety regulations. For these parts and their shipment, the supplier must obtain and retain a certificate of performance in accordance with appropriate government motor vehicle safety standards and regulations. Where mandatory, necessary instructions on the part drawing or engineering specification will be provided by Ford Motor Company's product engineering department.

Critical (∇) Characteristics

Those product or process characteristics that can affect compliance with government regulations or product safety functions are termed critical (∇) characteristics. Those products and processes identified as critical characteristics require special assembly, shipping, and monitoring, and they must be included in the supplier's quality control plan.

Set-Up Verification

This element requires the supplier to have machine or process set-up verification using statistical confirmation for all parts and processes with critical and significant characteristics

Control Item (∇) Fasteners

Those fasteners identified as control items must be controlled using the following special methods.

Material Analysis–Heat-Treated Parts—Before releasing a raw material for production of control item fasteners, a sample from each coil, rod, strip, or sheet metal must be analyzed and tested for conformance to chemical composition and quenching hardness requirements. The results of these tests must be recorded and must reference the heat number from the original steel mill.

Material Analysis–Nonheat-Treated Parts—The supplier must first visually check the identification tag of each coil of wire, rod, strip, or sheet metal to determine if the heat number complies with the mill analysis document and required specification. Then the supplier must test each raw material bundle for the required specific properties.

Lot Traceability—Each lot of control item fasteners must be traceable.

Heat Treating

This element requires that the supplier control all heat treatment processes according to *Ford Manufacturing Standard W-HTX-12*. Such processes will be audited according to *Ford Heat Treat System Survey Guidelines*. For parts identified as critical characteristics (∇), the heat treatment process must be controlled according to *Ford Manufacturing Standard W-HTX-1*. All heat-treated steel parts must also meet Ford Engineering Manual Specification WSS-M99A3-A.

Process Change and Design Changes for Supplier-Responsible Design

This element requires that all suppliers of control item (∇) parts or any part identified with "No change without prior approval" on the design record must obtain approval from Ford's product engineering function using Form 1638A: Supplier Request Form for Engineering Approval, which is available from Ford's purchasing department.

Supplier Modification of Control Item (∇) Requirements

Suppliers are always encouraged by Ford Motor Company to improve their products and processes. If supplier-provided control item materials and products show higher capability as evidenced by control charts and engineering specification test data, then the supplier may request a revision to the testing and inspection requirements for those parts from Ford's product engineering and quality function. The revised control plan must be approved prior to its implementation. If a product or process is subject to upstream control, then the supplier can request replacement of finished product inspection using a similar approach.

Engineering Specification (ES) Test Performance Requirements

When a product fails to pass engineering specifications, the supplier must immediately stop all production shipments of that product pending corrective action. The supplier should also immediately inform the customer of the test failure, halt shipments, and identify lot numbers of any suspect shipments. Any suspect product should be sorted thoroughly and repaired before any further shipment. The process must be analyzed to determine the root cause, and corrective action must be taken and documented. The supplier may resume shipment again only after the root cause(s) has been identified and corrected. Suspect product requires further sorting and reworking.

If the root cause of the failure is undetermined, then product engineering and the consumer location must be notified immediately that the product meets all other requirements except the engineering specification test. The supplier shall wait for further instructions before resuming production.

System Design Specification (SDS)

This element requires that the supplier compile and maintain records of performance measures for a system or subsystem using measurable characteristics from customer expectation data.

Ongoing Process Monitoring

This element requires that the supplier select appropriate methods such as SPC to monitor and control all dimensions and other product characteristics. For those characteristics that are not controlled by SPC or are not described in the control plan, the supplier should use either product audits on a regular basis, periodic product layout and laboratory tests, or *product qualification* for attribute characteristics according to Table A on page 67 per Ford-Specific Requirements in *Quality System Requirement: QS-9000*, published by the Automotive Industry Action Group. For product qualification, a sample of at least two hundred units must be checked to approve a lot of eights hour or one day of production. If twenty consecutive lots are found to have no defects, a sample size of fifty units may be used. Any time a nonconforming unit is found, the lot must be 100% inspected, the root cause found, and corrective action taken. For monitoring and controlling products using SPC, the most recent point on the control chart and the historical process capability index (Cpk) must be used to take appropriate action. The numerical value of the Cpk is calculated by using the engineering specification in the numerator and six times the standard deviation of the specification in the denominator. Ford has set the target value of the Cpk index at 1.33. If the process has a Cpk less than 1.33, then 100% must be inspected. For a Cpk between 1.33 and 1.67 or more, the product is acceptable but the supplier must continue to reduce the variation. For detailed information on SPC, refer to *Fundamental Statistical Process Control: Reference Manual*, published by the Automotive Industry Action Group.

Prototype Part Quality Initiatives

If the supplier is engaged in prototype building, then the proto-type vehicle construction data can be used for planning the production process. Prototype evaluation may be accomplished using Percent Inspection points which Satisfy Tolerance (PIST) and Percent Indices which are Process Capable (PIPC). PIST is the ratio of how many inspection points actually meet the specifications over the total number of points (characteristics) checked in the lot. PIPC is the ratio of how many Cpk characteristics of 1.33 or greater are present over the total number of characteristics checked.

Quality Operating System

The supplier is required to use Ford's Quality Operating System (QOS) concepts and methodology to achieve increased levels of customer satisfaction. QOS takes a systematic approach to total quality management using standardized tools and practices. Many levels of QOS may be developed across the supplier's organization. A number of small groups could be working on various problems and continuous quality improvement efforts, while a steering committee may meet periodically to evaluate the entire system. Evaluation of the supplier's QOS systems is currently performed by a Ford representative and the supplier's technical function according to the *QOS Assessment & Rating Procedure Manual*, published by Ford Motor Company.

Qualification and Acceptance Criteria for Materials

This element requires that the supplier use material specification requirements for initial qualification of materials to be used in production. The supplier is also required to develop a control plan for its ongoing production. The plan must be reviewed and approved by Ford's materials engineering activity. This approval must precede the production part approval submission. An *Engineering Materials Approved Source List* is maintained by Ford's materials engineering function as part of its Material and Toxicology System (MATS). Requests for approval for materials clearance status and alternate sources should be directed to Ford's materials engineering function via the purchasing department.

Ford Bibliography

Nine reference manuals which provide additional information are listed under this element. They are available to suppliers from Ford buyers or the Supplier Technical Assistance Office.

- *Manufacturing Standards for Heat Treating W-HTX-1 and W-HTX-12*

- *Packaging Guidelines for Production Parts,* Form 1750 and 1750 EU

- *Failure Mode and Effects Analysis Handbook*

- *A Quality, Reliability Primer*

- *QOS Assessment & Rating Procedure*

- *QOS: Quality Is the Name of the Game!*

- *Supplier Quality Improvement Guidelines for Prototypes*

- *Heat Treat System Survey Guidelines*

- *Team Oriented Problem Solving*

General Motors-Specific Requirements

This section lists the requirements to be met by suppliers to General Motors Corporation. There are four elements in this section.

General Procedures and Other Requirements

GM NAO suppliers must meet the additional requirements or guidelines as outlined in the GM North American publications listed below. For the latest revision and ordering information, contact Boise Cascade Office Products at 1-800-421-7676 or 1-810-758-5400. For specific questions on the content of any of these documents, contact the appropriate authority at the GM procurement function. All GM NAO suppliers are advised to verify at least annually that they are using the latest version of the following documents:

- *C4 Technology Program, GM–Supplier C4 Information,* January 1994 (GM 1825)—Assists suppliers in understanding and executing GM's C4 strategy

- *Key Characteristics Designation System*, September 1993 (GM 1805 QN)—Defines GM's approach to "special" characteristics

- *Supplier Submission of Material for Process Approval* (GP-4), October 1993 (GM1407)—Provides shipping procedures for all pilot parts

- *Problem Reporting and Resolution Procedure* (GP-5), October 1991 (GM 1746)

- *Supplier Submission of Match Check Material* (GP-6), February 1990 (GM 1689)—How to providing notification by purchasing division if required

- *Component Verification & Traceability Procedure* (GP-7), February 1993 (GM 1730)

- *Continuous Improvement Procedure* (GP-8), October 1993 (GM 1747)—Required of all suppliers; replaces part certification procedure

- *Evaluation and Accreditation of Supplier Test Facilities* (GPI 0), February 1990 (GM 1796)

- *Early Production Containment Procedure* (GP-12), November 1993 (GM 1920)—Required for all parts needing production approval

- *Traceability Identifier Requirements for Selected Components on Passenger and Light Truck Vehicles, Traceability Identifier Requirement* (TIR 15-300), July 1989 (GM1731)

- *Specifications for Part and Component Bar Codes ECV/VCVS*, February 1993 (GM 1737)

- *Procedure for Suppliers of Material for Prototype* (GP-11), October 1993 (GM 1820)—Required for all prototype parts

- *Packaging and Identification Requirements for Production Parts* (GM 1738), revised September 1989

- *Shipping/Parts Identification Label Standard* (GM 1724), revised January 1993

- *Shipping and Delivery Performance Requirements* (GM 1797), October 1989

There are two notes to this section:

Note 1: The Production Part Approval Process, September 1993 version of GP-3 formerly known as Supplier Submission of Material for Production Approval

Note 2: The Quality System Requirements is considered to be the General Quality Standard (GQS) by General Motors Corporation

QS-9000 Applicability

This element reinforces that *Quality System Requirements: QS-9000* is applicable to all suppliers contracted by GM.

Customer Approval of Control Plans

This element states that customer approval of control plans and reaction plans is waived for suppliers of GM Europe unless otherwise stated in the contractual agreement.

UPC Labeling For Commercial Service Applications

This element states that GM Service Parts Operations (SPO) requires its suppliers to use UPC labeling rather than AIAG labeling for certain commercial applications. For further instructions in this matter, contact a GM service parts buyer.

Specific Requirements for Truck Manufacturers (Freightliner Corporation, Mack Trucks, Inc., Navistar International Transportation Corp., PACCAR Inc., Volvo GM Heavy Truck Corporation)

The above-mentioned truck manufacturers were actively involved in developing *Quality System Requirements: QS-9000*. They not only participated in but also adopted QS-9000 as their fundamental quality system requirements. For additional requirements, each individual truck manufacturer's publication must be referred to. To request any publication or information, contact the truck manufacturer's purchasing department.

HOW TO READ AND INTERPRET THE STANDARD

Within the context of *Quality System Requirements: QS-9000*, various phrases are used to address distinct grades of requirements. The majority of the sections have a *"shall"* clause, which in reality means that *those requirements must be accomplished.* Other less restrictive phrases are *"where appropriate," "where practical," "or other suitable means,"* etc. Other key advisory sentences include *"...where the absence of such instructions would affect quality," "inspect, test, and identify product as required by the quality plan or documented procedures,"* and so on. In fact, the difficulty in implementing the QS-9000 quality assurance system lies in the interpretation of its many subsections. At first glance, it appears to be very difficult to interpret their content. The paucity of precise instructions on what to do and how to do it can frustrate a quality manager who has to translate the generic sentence structure of the standards into a quality assurance system.

Unlike other supplier evaluation schemes, the standards do not impose a particular procedure and/or technique on a supplier. The document is intended to be a model or set of guidelines, but this suggests that the guidelines may be interpreted differently by each individual company. The weakness here is that there can be as many interpretations as there are readers and assessors. For example, Section 4.1.1 Quality Policy states, "The supplier's management shall define and document its policy and objectives for, and commitment to, quality. The supplier shall ensure that this policy is understood, implemented, and maintained at all levels in the organization." A company can address the issue of a quality policy by issuing a one-page statement supposedly written and signed by the CEO. The policy might be framed and displayed in various offices, but that certainly is not enough. As far as the standard is concerned, the policy must be *understood, implemented, and maintained at all levels in the organization.* The most important issue, then, is not necessarily having a policy but rather making sure (perhaps via training) that the policy is *practiced at all levels in the organization.*

The questions most often asked regarding a section are: "How do I do it?" and "What are the important points?" For example, Subsection 4.5.1 Document and Data Control states, "The supplier shall establish and maintain procedures to control all documents and data that relate to the requirements of this standard. These documents shall be reviewed and approved for adequacy by authorized personnel prior to issue." A quality manager may simply rephrase or slightly edit this subsection and include it in the company's quality manual without actually establishing and maintaining any such procedures. If procedures are written arbitrarily, third-party assessors will have no difficulty pointing out nonconformance during the audit. The strategy is not to write lengthy and detailed procedures, but to adapt current procedures to fit the requirements as per the standard. One approach might be to rephrase the subsection as a series of questions. For example, for paragraph 4.5.1, you could begin by asking: "Do we have procedures for controlling documents and data?" If the answer is no, you will either have to write some or come up with a pretty good reason to explain why you do not. Other questions might include: "How are documents/procedures approved?" and "Who approves procedural changes?" You may find that procedures do exist but that no one follows them. While it may be tempting to include layers of detailed instructions in the procedures, remember that they will be affected by changes and must be revised, updated, rewritten, signed, and approved. Therefore, it is better to keep the procedures as simple and straightforward as possible.

CONCLUSION

The preceding overview is not intended to be a substitute for actually reading *Quality System Requirements: QS-9000*. Anyone seriously considering implementing a QS-9000 quality assurance system should procure and review the original document in detail.

Satisfying each section of QS-9000 involves a substantial amount of preparation. A company planning to adapt its quality system to the QS-9000 model will still have to address each subsection, many of which are interrelated. Many companies try to accomplish this using a modular approach. However, if the interrelationship between subsections is ignored, a modular approach may fail to break the barriers that normally exist among departmental fortresses.

Establishing and maintaining quality records is certainly an important aspect of the standards. In general, most companies already have good to fair record keeping. All they need to do is make sure that the location of all records is identified and that pertinent records are kept up to date, reviewed as needed, properly archived, and retained for a predetermined period of time.

Suppose a company decides to make all of its laboratory procedures available electronically in an effort to reduce paperwork. Authorized parties would be able to easily update the centralized procedure files and quickly transmit them to all interested parties via electronic mail. Because all customers must be informed of (lab) process changes, the purchasing manager, on the other hand, would be faced with the enormous task of informing every customer, via official correspondence, of each and every change and/or modification. Thus, paperwork eliminated by one department could simply become a burden to another.

Therefore, the key questions to be answered are:

- Which standard is most appropriate?

- Which segment of the organization will have to be registered?

- How should we proceed and organize our efforts for the registration process?

3

QS-9000 QUALITY ASSURANCE SYSTEM

A quality assurance system refers to the organizational structure for formally documenting the responsibility and authority of the personnel in charge of quality assurance across the whole organization; documented policies, procedures, and work instructions; and the resources for implementing quality management. The quality assurance system, commonly known as the quality system, typically applies to and interacts with all activities that influence the quality of products or services offered by an organization. It applies to all stages, from initial identification to final satisfaction of customer needs and meeting requirements of standards. The goal of QS-9000 is the development of a quality system that will provide for continuous improvement with emphasis on prevention of defects and reduction of variation and waste in all production and distribution activities. The quality system of an organization also aims to accomplish the objectives of the organization in terms of its products or services. Therefore, a quality system may vary from one organization to another. However, the scope of a quality system covers both *product* and *service* elements of the customer–supplier relationship. Therefore, on-time delivery, correct invoicing, complaint resolution, etc. are all part of the quality system.

REQUIREMENTS OF THE QUALITY ASSURANCE SYSTEM

Section 4.0 of ISO 9001, ANSI/ASQC Q91, and *Quality System Requirements: QS-9000* (of which ISO 9001 is the core) require that the supplier must document and demonstrate that a formal quality system is in place and provide an authoritative description of the system. A commonly accepted way to document the organization of a quality system is through the preparation of a quality manual. The quality manual is considered to be the directory of the quality system. It should address three fundamental elements—*quality policy, quality management,* and the *quality system*—in order to achieve quality.

Quality Policy

The supplier's top management shall develop and document a quality policy statement which defines the overall quality objectives and direction of the organization as they pertain to key elements of quality such as performance, safety, and reliability, as formally expressed by top management. The quality policy may also contain the mission statement and such guidelines as are necessary to demonstrate the supplier's commitment to quality. The policy statement must be signed and dated by the CEO and included in the quality manual. The supplier's management is responsible for communicating the quality policy across the organization and reinforcing it thoroughly. Just writing a policy statement and incorporating it into the quality manual is not enough; the policy must be understood, implemented, and maintained at all levels of the organization.

Quality Management

Quality management includes the overall management function that establishes and implements the quality policy across the organization. Top management must clearly define the responsibilities, authority, and interfaces of the quality management. An organization chart is often used to define responsible functions and critical interfaces of personnel used to perform quality-related activities. Individuals responsible for quality-related actions must have the independence and the authority to carry out those actions in a timely manner.

Quality System

A quality system is the organizational structure, responsibilities, procedures, processes, and resources used for implementing quality management. It includes all activities pertinent to the quality of products and services offered by the organization. In order to successfully implement a quality system, an organization must recognize that its quality policy, quality management, and quality system are symbiotically linked to each other in a logical hierarchical network. Most implementation failures are generally attributable to situations where the quality policy either refutes the importance of or downplays the need for management's commitment to quality and/or cases where the quality system is hastily organized and adopted without the knowledge, support, or consent of those directly involved or affected.

TOTAL QUALITY MANAGEMENT AND QS-9000 MODEL

When an organization begins to implement a QS-9000 quality assurance system, a vast network of customer–supplier relationships begins to develop. When done properly and in a spirit of cooperation, it can lead to a sharing and exchange of information across previously impermeable departmental barriers. The phenomenon is similar to total quality management (TQM). The quality system requirements in QS-9000 are designed to ensure that a series of steps are taken so that the supplier indeed satisfies its customer's requirements. Although registration to QS-9000 requires a significant amount of documentation, which may unveil a multitude of problems that have accumulated over the years, it does not guarantee TQM or the production of quality products. TQM is a system-wide effort for achieving quality in producing products. Third-party registration to QS-9000 is simply an accreditation process to ensure that the supplier meets the quality requirements of the customer according to their contractual agreement. However, TQM can be designed and implemented by incorporating the quality system requirements of QS-9000 and/or other standards which pertain to the requirements of the customer and the industry.

SCOPE AND APPLICATION OF QS-9000 REGISTRATION

A large number of suppliers to the big three automakers have expressed an interest in QS-9000 registration simply because their customers have requested, demanded, or otherwise indicated that it will be a requirement in the near future. QS-9000 is aimed primarily at detecting and preventing nonconformances during the production, distribution, and installation stages and the implementation of a quality system by the supplier to prevent their recurrence. In essence, QS-9000 is nothing more than a set of requirements which should be in place whenever two parties enter into a contractual agreement. Therefore, before embarking on documentation efforts, it is important for a company to determine the exact contractual arrangements regarding product quality and evaluate its basic contractual philosophy which applies to the majority of its clients. This will help the company determine how to answer some of the questions it may have regarding QS-9000 registration. As early as possible, it is advisable that a company develop a flowchart of the contractual processes with the help of the people involved in contract review. This will be very helpful in the later stages of the implementation plan. One of the most important tasks during the implementation stage is to collect, identify, sort, and validate all available documents. Then, it is necessary to determine to which tier each document belongs and which QS-9000 section or subsection it addresses. Suppliers that already maintain an effective quality system, such as companies that currently comply with their customers' supplier quality assurance systems, have found that the majority of their available documentation satisfies the QS-9000 quality system requirements.

Table 3.1 Questions for QS-9000 Registration

- Why QS-9000 registration? What are its goal, purpose, and objectives?
- Which QS-9000 standard—9001, 9002, or 9003?
- Which product or product line(s)?
- Which plant(s) or portion of the plant to register?
- Are the plants or functions geographically separated? If so, how will they be coordinated?
- How should we proceed? Should we register one pilot plant first and then other plants or register all plants simultaneously?
- What resources are available?
- What is the timetable for implementation?
- What level of commitment do we have?
- Is it necessary to coordinate our efforts with other organizations, such as OSHA?
- Are there any internal subcontractors that should be registered? If so, who and when? Which QS-9000 standard (9001, 9002, or 9003) should they be required to register under?
- Are there any external subcontractors that should be registered? If so, who and when? Which QS-9000 standard (9001, 9002, or 9003) applies to them?

In some companies, the existing organizational structure may be quite different from the implicit structure delineated within the QS-9000 guidelines. Process ownership and document control, for example, may not be clearly delineated or may not follow a linear flow. This raises a number of questions, as listed in Table 3.1.

CONCLUSION

Because top management's commitment to the quality policy is critical to the success of the implementation process, it is important to answer the questions listed in Table 3.1 before organizing a quality assurance system to facilitate the registration procedure.

It is important to know whether top management is seriously committed to QS-9000 registration. Without top management's commitment, it is impossible to achieve QS-9000 registration. It is also important to determine which plant or function will be registered and to which standard (9001, 9002, or 9003). Especially in situations where an organization is geographically and functionally decentralized, where R&D maintains documentation in strict secrecy from manufacturing functions, and where overseas operations are involved, it is critical to determine up front which operations should seek QS-9000 registration. Aiming for total organization-wide QS-9000 registration in such cases could be quite impractical. Once these questions have been answered, a supplier can start to organize its quality assurance system.

4

DOCUMENTING A QS-9000 QUALITY ASSURANCE SYSTEM

Quality System Requirements: QS-9000 requires that the quality system be documented to demonstrate that a formally organized quality system is in place. This not only means that the elements of the quality system must be adequate, but it also ensures that product or service conformity complies with the specified requirements of the standards. An accepted means of documenting the quality system is through a quality manual, descriptions of quality-related procedures, quality system auditing reports, and other quality records. The quality manual is the directory of the quality system. It should describe the quality policy, specify quality-related responsibilities, and identify quality-related procedures. The quality manual may be corporate or divisional, or it may address a specific function or process within a plant site. The quality manual must define the scope of the quality system it addresses.

A PYRAMID MODEL WITH THREE-TIERED DOCUMENTATION

Documentation of a QS-9000 quality system may use the concept of a pyramid model with three-tiered documentation, as shown in Figure 4.1. This is a generic approach which has evolved over the years, and it should not be construed as being required by QS-9000 standards. Although no requirements specify or even outline how the quality system should be organized, many experts and registrars seem to strongly suggest that one efficient way to organize a quality system is to adopt the three-tiered pyramid model. This structure recognizes three types of documents. Tier one includes the *quality manual,* tier two includes *quality procedures,* and tier three includes all *work instructions and quality records.* These documents must be prepared with reference to QS-9000 quality system requirements and other customer reference manuals, such as *Advanced Product Quality Planning and Control Plan, Failure Mode*

FIGURE 4.1 A Pyramid Model with Three-Tiered Documentation

and Effects Analysis, Measurement Systems Analysis, and *Fundamental Statistical Process Control.*

Tier One: The Quality Manual

Almost all third-party registrars require that a quality manual be written and submitted for registration. Although consultants and auditors do not always agree as to what constitutes a model quality manual, most would agree that it should address each of the QS-9000 sections and subsections. Of course, there is flexibility in terms of design, style, content, page format, control policies, and other related issues. As a document, the manual should be brief and concise. The purpose of the quality manual is to assure the assessor that the company has indeed addressed all of the relevant QS-9000 sections and subsections. How each department addresses each task is detailed in departmental procedures which belong to tier two documentation, which in turn might refer to tier three detailed work instructions. Contrary to traditional practices of documenting a quality system, QS-9000 requires that the detailed documentation of procedures and work instructions not be a part of the quality manual.

The Format of a Quality Manual

Regardless of style, the quality manual should have a particular format. A sample format for a quality manual is presented in Appendix A. This format is generally accepted by most leading registrars. The format of a quality manual must include the following:

- The *name of the company* or *the plant* must appear at the top of each page (or at least on the title page).
- A *table of contents* must follow the title page.
- A *document control box* must be inserted at the bottom of each page.
- A *revision list* page must be included just after the *table of contents* page.

- *A distribution list* page must follow the *revision list* page.

Note: The manual may be borrowed or reviewed by anyone and therefore may not always reside permanently at one particular location. However, the person in charge of the manual is responsible for the manual at his or her location.

A common tendency is to include too much detailed information, such as laboratory procedures, technical specifications, and names of individuals responsible for specific tasks. Such detailed information should not be inserted in the quality manual. Similarly, inclusion of information which changes very often, such as names of managers, is not advised because every time there is a change in such information, an updated version of the quality manual will have to be issued. Table 4.1 lists some of the important questions that may be asked while preparing the quality manual.

TABLE 4.1 Questions For Preparing a Quality Manual

- To whom will the quality manual be distributed (distribution list)?
- By whom and how will the revisions be made?
- How will the document be controlled?
- Who will make sure that obsolete quality manuals are removed from circulation?
- Who will be responsible for addressing the Management Responsibility section?
- Who will write the quality manual?
- How will the task of coordinating all the sections be addressed?
- How will we ensure that no unreasonable claims have been made throughout the manual?
- Who will be responsible for reviewing and approving the manual for accuracy prior to final release? (A suggestion would be to include everyone on the distribution list.)
- What should be included in the control box?

Some quality manuals developed by some agencies are so generic and preformatted that they can be modified on a word processor to suit any client's need. Some companies market a "quality manual software package," where the user only has to input only a few key words, choose a style, and select one of many scenarios and the software will take care of the rest. However, as a word of caution, before purchasing such a generic quality manual or software package, it is important to make sure that it will fit your company's need.

A typical quality manual format consists of three distinct sections: *scope, policy,* and *responsibilities.*

In the *scope* section, the author of the quality manual basically presents an overview of the general procedures the organization has designed to achieve product quality and the purpose of the quality manual.

The *policy* section describes, in very general terms, the actual company policy. This section may include a number of subsections to describe the company's quality policy, confirm the CEO's commitment to the stated quality policy, and ensure that the procedures stated in the quality manual are enforced.

The *responsibility* section explains who (without specifically naming anyone) is responsible for quality by department, process, and/or activity. Table 4.2 provides a list of information to be included in the quality manual. At the same time, a responsibility matrix (displayed in Table 4.3) may be used to delegate responsibility for developing, documenting, and enforcing procedures in accordance with QS-9000 criteria.

Sometimes quality manuals merely rephrase the standard. This is not to imply that such a style should be avoided. In fact, many U.S. multinational corporations with subsidiaries in Europe tend to adopt the quality manuals of their European plants with only minor modifications.

There can literally be as many styles as there are writers. Quality manuals written by outside consultants tend to be more generic than those written by staff members. The style and format of subcontracted quality manuals are sometimes too elaborate, too voluminous, and look too perfect. If such a document is adopted by a small manufacturer, it may arouse suspicion as to who owns the document. After all, the quality manual, whether developed

Table 4.2 Information for Inclusion in a Quality Manual

- A policy statement from the highest corporate officer, stating that the quality assurance system described in the quality manual represents the company's commitment to quality and the policy

- . Delegation of responsibility and authority to some department (such as the quality assurance department) for developing, documenting, and enforcing the quality assurance system

- Assignment of responsibilities to each department within the organization for developing and implementing procedures and necessary work instructions to support their designated activities

- Description of how the company is organized using an organization chart

- Matrix of departmental responsibilities versus requirements of standards

- An outline of the three-tiered documentation that governs the quality system

- A glossary of terms, including definitions and acronyms unique to the company

Table 4.3 Typical Responsibility Matrix

ISO 9001- Based Criteria	Pres.	V.P. Operations	V.P. Mktg.	V.P. Finance
4.1.2.1 Responsibility & Authority				
4.1.2.2 Verification Resources				
4.1.2.3 Management Representative				
4.1.3 Management Review				
... ...				
... ...				
... ...				
4.18 Training				
4.20 Statistical Techniques				

by a staff member or an outside contractor, must reflect the reality of the company's quality assurance system.

Some companies distribute their quality manuals to their suppliers on write-protected diskettes. Although this process can be very effective, many registrars are not sufficiently electronically sophisticated to accept diskettes from potential clients.

Some companies seem to want to copyright their manuals. Although there may be some need to protect certain sensitive documents, a QS-9000 quality manual does not have to be copyrighted. The information contained in the manual is generally made available to all potential customers. Therefore, the content of the quality manual should be generic in nature and should not reveal any sensitive information. If any sensitive information is to be included, it should appear in tier two or tier three documents and not in the quality manual.

Tier Two: Departmental Procedures

Departmental procedures typically form the second-tier documents. They are designed and developed to address the quality assurance system in each department within the organization. Typically, these procedures address all QS-9000 criteria and other criteria pertinent to contractual agreements. These procedures are interdepartmental in nature and deal with the general flow and control of processes across the company. They describe each activity, who is responsible, when it has to be done, where it will occur, and how it will be carried out. The amount of detail covered in the procedures depends on the size and needs of the company and the nature of its products and quality-related activities. An internal audit program must be installed as a part of the procedures to determine whether they conform to the overall quality system.

Departmental procedures can be beneficial if internal customers/suppliers are given the opportunity to review them in order to learn about each other's perceived responsibilities. The quality manual and procedures are generally two sets of documents. Each department usually generates its own set of departmental procedures. These documents should be more detailed than the tier one document. Table 4.4 provides a list of information to be included in departmental procedures.

Table 4.4   Information to Be Included in Departmental Procedures

- Explanation of the department's functions

- An organization chart of the department, briefly describing everyone's responsibility, authority, and functions

- The appropriate standard operating procedures

- A list of the department's internal and/or external suppliers and customers (this is optional but very valuable information which can easily be described using flow diagrams)

Most consultants prefer to organize tier two documents by simply following each of the QS-9000 sections and subsections referred to in tier one and explaining each item in greater detail, such as who controls a process, who is responsible for instrument calibration, who performs final product inspection, etc. This approach may be applicable for small plants but may not be suitable for large plants, particularly when several departments are responsible for the same or similar activities, such as document control and instrument calibration (i.e., metrology). Many companies address document control in a corporate or plant policy statement instead of writing a unique document control procedure for each department. Similarly, some plants have as many as four or five organizations performing calibration of measuring equipment, depending on the type of instrumentation. Instead of each organization writing its own calibration procedure, a common calibration procedure document could be produced. On the other hand, many companies prefer that each department prepare its own tier two documentation as long as duplication of effort is avoided. It is important to make sure that the procedure is properly implemented, because an auditor will want to know if everyone involved with document control is aware of the procedure and its many steps. The format for a departmental procedure provided in Appendix B is generally accepted by most third-party registrars, although many other formats and styles are available. As of yet, however, no standards have been established for how to write procedures.

Tier Three: Work Instructions

Work instructions are very specific instructions related to work that might affect production, assembly, operation, installation, etc. They provide step-by-step information on how to perform a specific task and are interdepartmental in nature. Work instructions are also known as *operating practices*. They must be written in such a way that they will be understood by the lowest level employee qualified to perform that task. How much and what to write are the two major questions facing those in charge of writing work instructions. Inspection instructions, testing instructions, calibration instructions, purchase order preparation instructions, schedule preparation instruction, production material requisition instructions, etc. are some typical examples of work instructions. A format for work instructions is provided in Appendix B.

GUIDELINES FOR WRITING PROCEDURES AND WORK INSTRUCTIONS

Some effective guidelines for writing procedures and work instructions are listed below.

1. Read the corresponding QS-9000 subsection and verify if any other sections are cross-referenced. For example, Subsection 4.18 Training of ISO-Based Requirements cross-references Subsection 4.1.6 Quality Record and Subsection 4.1.2.2 Verification Resources and Personnel.

2. Rephrase each sentence of the subsection into a series of questions. For example, after reading all the relevant subsections in Section 4.18, ask, "Is this pertinent to our industry?" The answer should be yes because Section 4.18 applies to any industry. Then ask the following set of questions:

> "What procedures are currently in place to identify training needs and provide training for all personnel who perform activities that affect quality?"

> "Are training records maintained properly?"

"Who can help us answer the above questions (e.g., human resources, supervisors, others)?"

3. If no or inadequate procedures or records exist, decide who should revise or write some simple and easily implemented procedures.

4. Avoid vague statements, as they may generate a number of other questions from an auditor.

5. Avoid statements that seem to refer to an existing problem, as they may create doubt about the existing procedure in the mind of the auditor. Suppose a procedure contains the following statement: "Failure of the oxygen pump seal has occurred in the past and created a hazardous problem. The operator should be aware at all times that a leak can occur, and in such situations the operator must shut the pump down until the problem is identified and corrected." Such a statement may trigger a number of questions in the mind of the auditor, such as:

"What is wrong with that procedure?"

"Why has the problem not been corrected and the operation made safe?"

6. Avoid writing a manual or procedure that merely rephrases some of the QS-9000 subsections. For example, instead of writing, "This training must be provided by individuals..." (an obvious paraphrasing of ISO), simply write, "Training is provided by qualified individuals." Of course, qualified individuals must be defined (e.g., months or years of experience, certification, special training, etc.).

7. The documentation of procedures and work instructions need not always be elaborate. If a procedure becomes too complex and requires input from several individuals, it should be broken down into a number of subprocedures.

8. If there is more than one way to operate a process, it must be stated in the procedures.

9. For some processes, documenting each and every possible option could require many more procedures, some of which would rarely be used. In such cases, the Pareto principle may be used. Generally, a few procedures usually cover 85% of all possible actions. These are standard procedures.

10. In some cases (15 or 20% of the time) where deviation from standard procedures may occur, briefly explain the deviating procedure(s) and who the operator should contact for each deviation. Maintenance instructions are examples of such complex procedures. Maintenance crews often claim that they do not have time to maintain detailed records. They need not maintain any detailed records if a checklist is prepared and maintained. Such records can be invaluable for preventive maintenance and can be used for estimating mean time between failure or detecting breakdown patterns.

FLOWCHARTING A PROCEDURE

One common way to document a procedure is to create a flowchart. A flowchart is a schematic representation of a process or procedure using symbols. Generally, a square denotes an operation or task, a circle denotes an inspection, an inverted triangle denotes storage, a diamond indicates a decision point (yes or no), an arrow indicates the flow of materials and documentation, and a rounded rectangle indicates some delay in the process. An example of a flowchart is provided in Appendix B.

The following steps are generally recommended for flowcharting a process or procedure:

1. Define the boundaries of the process or procedure.

2. Make sure that all persons responsible for the process or procedure are present.

3. Interview all responsible persons, write down what they say, and have them review what you write to make sure that you have written down what they actually do.

4. Flowchart the process or procedure.

5. Review and make final improvements.

6. Determine how often the procedure applies.

7 Determine how the procedure operates (i.e., technical issues).

8. Determine if it is a key procedure which affects product quality.

A flowchart can also be used as a tool for work simplification analysis. It helps in locating process control mechanisms, such as inspection points, and is useful in identifying process bottlenecks. To an auditor, an assembly flowchart provides a picture of what might be experienced during a long tour through the assembly line. A flowchart is also a convenient place to record information, observations, etc. made during the tour of the assembly line. An auditor can also study location and extent of control to determine whether they are in compliance with requirements. A flowchart also allows for continuous improvement in process effectiveness.

CONCLUSION

There is no standard style or format for writing procedures and work instructions. The author can be as creative and detailed as he or she wishes, as long as what is written is indeed what is done. At the same time, there is no need to write procedures for everything. In some plants, detailed work instructions have been automated or effective computerization of control procedures has been implemented, which allows the process engineer to monitor a process for as many as a dozen or more parameters. All these procedures are acceptable as long as they are used effectively by operators or process engineers to monitor product quality.

5

PREPARATION
FOR QS-9000
REGISTRATION

Before seeking QS-9000 registration, a number of questions must be answered and much preparation must take place. Many companies tend to rush toward registration and, to their disappointment, encounter countless nagging difficulties. Failure to plan for, prepare for, and anticipate problems can lead to unnecessary and frustrating delays. Table 5.1 provides a list of questions that must be asked by the QS-9000 committee before proceeding with QS-9000 registration.

DEVELOPING A RESPONSIBILITY MATRIX

At first, it is important to decide which product lines, plants, or divisions will be registered and who will be responsible for ISO implementation. Although responsibility usually falls to the quality manager/director, it needs to be shared with many others, including the highest ranking executive. Such sharing of respon-

TABLE 5.1   List of Questions for QS-9000 Registration Preparation

- Who will be responsible for the implementation effort?
- How will the employees be informed about the company's plan for QS-9000 registration?
- Which plants, divisions, or product lines will be registered?
- Who will be responsible for which QS-9000 subsections? (Use a responsibility matrix for this purpose.)
- Who (in-house team, consultant, or combination) will perform the pre-assessment audit, and when it will be carried out?
- Who will write the quality manual and who will review it ? Will it be written by a single individual or will various persons be assigned to write different sections?
- Who will write tier two and tier three documents?
- Who will manage document control? Which documents need to be controlled?
- Who will conduct the internal audit? How will it be conducted?
- How will training needs be accomplished?

sibility indicates a total commitment to quality. One way to assign responsibilities is by preparing a responsibility matrix, as shown in Table 5.2.

PRE-ASSESSMENT AUDIT

A pre-assessment audit is also important to determine how a company is currently prepared and how long it will approximately take to implement QS-9000. The pre-assessment audit is usually carried out by an in-house team, a consultant, or both. If an in-house team is used, the team first elects a lead assessor. The best candidate is probably the quality manager/director. The lead assessor then plans the audit, decides how he or she will proceed, and determines who will ask which questions. He or she also explains the purpose of the audit to the auditee, emphasizing that

TABLE 5.2 Responsibility Matrix

Subsection	Quality Plant Manager	Operation Manager	Purchasing Manager	Lab Manager	Research Manager	Marketing Develop.	Others Manager	Manager
4.1.1 Quality Policy								
4.1.2 Organization								
4.1.2.2 Verif. Resource								
4.1.2.3 Mgt. Repr.								
4.1.3 Mgt. Review								
4.2 Quality System								
4.3 Contract Review								
4.4 Design Control								
4.5 Document Control								
4.6 Purchasing								
4.6.2 Evaluation								
...								
...								
4.20 Statistical Tech.								

this is an exploratory audit designed to determine how much effort will be required to implement QS-9000. This audit involves a series of interviews which follow a questionnaire. A pre-assessment audit questionnaire may be prepared in accordance with *Quality System Assessment (QSA)*, a set of audit guidelines published by the Automotive Industry Action Group.

RESPONSIBILITY FOR WRITING QUALITY MANUALS AND PROCEDURES

The next step is to determine who will write the quality manual, the quality procedures, and the work instructions. The quality manager/director usually writes the quality manual. This responsibility must be shared with the CEO, which shows top management's commitment to quality. It is essential that the highest ranking executive at least review and approve the final version of the manual. This can be documented by having each page of the manual signed by the CEO or the plant manager. Once the final version has been edited, the manual should be submitted to the president for final editing and approval. The quality manual documents a company's quality system. Therefore, prior to its release, it must be reviewed by each division directly affected by its content. A distribution list, which includes the approval signature of all directors/managers involved with the content, must be attached to the quality manual. This distribution list will become a part of the manual. The quality manual is generally circulated among departments/divisions in order to allow everyone to participate, communicate, or otherwise share in the development and formalization of the company's quality system. It also allows for the coordination of efforts among divisions and the coordination of tier one and tier two documentation. Therefore, a circulation list must also be maintained in order to locate the manual at any time.

Tier two documentation can be developed by either the quality manager/director or someone to whom he or she has delegated the job. On the other hand, using the internal supplier/customer model, a department/division can develop its own tier two documentation and have its internal supplier(s) verify the procedures. Writing of tier three documents can be delegated to supervisors or even operators. A convenient way to develop tier two and tier three documents would be to have them written by one individual and verified by the appropriate managers/ supervisors.

In preparing tier two and tier three documentation, only what currently is being done should be written; what should be done or will be done in the future should not be included. This does not mean that continuous improvement is not part of the QS-9000 registration process; on the contrary, it merely suggests that what currently is being done should be documented first in order to meet the registration requirements. Attempting to do everything at once can reduce the chance of success in obtaining registration.

DEVELOPING DOCUMENT CONTROL

Document control is an important QS-9000 registration requirement. Documents such as the quality manual, procedures, work instructions, quality records, etc. must be controlled. This responsibility must be assigned to one or more persons. At the same time, a document control procedure must be established as part of the QS-9000 requirements (Section 4.16 of ISO 9001-based requirements and Section 4.15 of ISO 9002-based requirements).

ESTABLISHING INTERNAL AUDITING

An internal audit is an important control element of the quality system. It can be conducted by consultants or by an internal audit team, which must consist of qualified and trained auditors. A procedure must be written for conducting internal audits, the frequency of such audits, documentation of audit records, and corrective actions. The procedure should also address the training requirements for verification resource personnel (Subsection 4.1.2.2 of ISO 9001-based requirements). It is also important to address the training needs of all personnel whose work affects quality (Section 4.18 of ISO 9001-based requirements).

Finally, it is necessary to develop a preliminary timetable for QS-9000 implementation. Pre-assessment audit information would be very helpful for this purpose. Once developed, the timetable must be updated as often as is necessary.

PREPARING A TIMETABLE FOR QS-9000 REGISTRATION

The time needed to implement a quality assurance system that conforms to the QS-9000 model generally depends on the size of the company, the commitment of top management to achieve registration by a certain date, the expertise of the consultant in guiding the client, the amount of documentation required, availability of qualified and trained personnel to prepare the documentation, the type and degree of resistance against the effort from various organizations, the number of individuals and groups involved, and other intangibles factors.

A company with approximately two hundred employees that has only a rudimentary quality system in place generally needs about six to nine months to bring its quality system up to QS-9000 standards. Most companies, if seriously committed, can achieve the task within nine to fifteen months. Assuming that a company is seriously committed, the rule of thumb would be to allow twenty-five to thirty working days for the actual writing of the quality manual, although many more (twelve to sixteen) weeks may be needed to decide what to include in it. One-half to a full day should be allowed for the writing of each tier two document, although these activities can be spread over twelve to sixteen weeks. Tier three documentation takes about one day to write and one day to edit, spread over twelve to sixteen weeks. Internal audits and corrective actions can take anywhere from forty to fifty days, depending on plant size and the number of nonconformities found when auditing and testing the system. These estimates assume that a company is totally committed to the task and is willing to invest the necessary resources in order to achieve QS-9000 registration within a reasonable time frame of nine to fifteen months. However, these estimates do not include any training or preparation time. Training can easily lengthen the registration process and increase the cost significantly. Technical and quality-related training sessions are required for QS-9000 registration and are also required by other agencies such as OSHA and EPA. Such training is very expensive and can consume as much as 70% of the allocated budget. These training programs must be carefully timed and should be practical rather than theoretical in order to be effective.

Table 5.3 provides an overview of a QS-9000 implementation plan for a hypothetical company with approximately two hundred employees.

A company seeking registration should be stable and not undergoing any reorganization. Companies that are in the midst of

TABLE 5.3 QS-9000 Implementation Plan for a Hypothetical Company

- Initiate QS-9000 awareness campaign
  Establish implementation timetable
  Communicate the QS-9000 implementation plan across the organization
- Nominate QS-9000 coordinator(s) and delegate authority and responsibilities
- Establish implementation teams
  Assign responsibility for writing quality manual and procedures
- Start writing quality manual
  Review QS-9000 guidelines
- Coordinate with procedure teams
- Develop process flowchart
  Flowchart processes as needed
- Document procedures (tier two)
- Document work instructions (tier three)
- Set up quality audit training according to QS-9000 standards
- Set up pre-registration audit
- Monitor the implementation process
  Start internal audits
  Document corrective actions
- Schedule a compliance audit
- Clear up any discrepancies
- QS-9000 registration

a major or even a minor restructuring can anticipate a much longer implementation time period.

The purpose of the quality awareness campaign is to inform the work force why the company wants to achieve QS-9000 registration within a certain period of time. A one- or two-day in-house QS-9000 awareness seminar can be a very effective way to inform the work force, as opposed to sending one or two representatives to one of the many QS-9000 seminars available. A well-planned informative campaign is the most effective way to achieve this awareness.

The next step is to appoint the QS-9000 representatives and teams whose purpose will be to organize, monitor, catalyze, and energize the implementation process, including the assignment of tier one, tier two, and tier three documentation. Then the entire process has to be constantly monitored to ensure effective and steady progress.

As the process progresses, the time will come (in about six months) to conduct the first *internal audits*. This is a critical step in the implementation process. Most third-party registrars will not even bother to audit a company until its quality assurance system has been in place for at least six months. In the meantime, an ongoing quality training program must be in place to train the quality verification personnel and the personnel whose activities impact product quality.

If the pre-registration audit reveals any noncompliances, corrective actions must be taken to eliminate those discrepancies. All corrective actions must be documented. Then a third-party auditor can be invited to officially assess the company's readiness. If everything goes well, the company can receive its registration certificate within a few months. Table 5.4 provides an overview of a QS-9000 implementation schedule for a company with approximately two hundred employees.

ESTIMATING THE COST OF QS-9000 REGISTRATION

Using the preliminary pre-assessment audit findings and the implementation schedule as guidelines, the cost of QS-9000 registration may be estimated. Without a preliminary audit, it is extremely

TABLE 5.4   QS-9000 Implementation Schedule for a Hypothetical Company

Year	Jan	Feb	Mar	Apr	May	Jun	Jul	Aug	Sep	Oct	Nov	Dec

XX
Awareness campaign

X
Nominate QS-9000 coordinators

XXXXXXXXXXXXXXXX
Write quality manual

XXXXXXXXXXXXXXXX
Write quality procedures

XXXXXXXXXXXXXXXXXXXX
Write work instructions

XXXXXXXXXXXXXXXXXXXXXXXXXXXXXXXXXXXXXXXXXXX
Set up and run quality training according to QS-9000 requirements

XX
Set up pre-registration audit

XXXXXXXXXXXXXXXXXXXXXXXXXXXXXXXXXXXXXXXXX
Monitor the implementation process

XXXXXXXXXX
Start internal audit

XXXXXXXXX
Corrective actions

XXXXXXXX
Third-party audit compliance

XXXXX
Clear up any discrepancies

XXXXXX
QS-9000 registration

difficult to estimate the cost of QS-9000 registration. A medium-sized company with two hundred employees can spend anywhere from $50,000 to $150,000 for QS-9000 registration, not including any training and preparation costs. There are too many variables with too many parameters to consider when estimating the cost of QS-9000 registration. Table 5.5 provides a model for estimating the cost of various activities related to QS-9000 registration based on 1995 estimates for a company with approximately two hun-

TABLE 5.5. Model for Estimating Various QS-9000 Registration-Related Costs Using Values Based Upon 1995 Estimates for Companies with Approximately Two Hundred Employees

Item	Rate	Average Time	Average Cost
ISO quality manual	$40/hr*	150 man-hrs	$6,000
ISO quality procedures	$40/hr*	200 man-hrs	$8,000
ISO work instructions	$40/hr*	250 man-hrs	$10,000
Internal audit + corrective actions	$50/hr*	100 man-hrs	$5,000
Pre-assessment audit (third party)	$1,500/au/day	4 au-days	$6,000
Certification audit (third party)	$1,500/au/day	10 au-days	$15,000
Average total one-time cost (excluding preparation and ongoing training costs)			$50,000
Training quality resource personnel	$100/hr	1,000 man-hrs	$100,000
Registration fee	Variable	N/A	
Semi-annual surveillance audit	$1,500/au/day	4 au-days/yr	$6,000/yr

* Estimated from salary + benefits.

dred employees. These cost and time estimates are based on the assumption that a company is committed to the QS-9000 registration process.

QS-9000 registration costs, of course, vary from company to company. The majority of the costs are associated with documentation, audits, and training. According to a recent survey on ISO 9000 registration by Dusharme (1995), registrars charge from $5,000 to $10,000 for a pre-assessment audit, $10,000 to $45,000 for a registration audit, and $5,000 to $15,000 for a surveillance audit. The survey also reports that an initial documentation review can cost from $6,000 to $18,000, while the internal cost for documentation and training can range from $100,000 to $150,000. Software is available for documentation and training, which can speed up the documentation and training processes. The survey also reports that consultants charge from $800 to $2,000 per day, and consulting costs for a company can range from $20,000 to $50,000. Although this information was reported for ISO 9000 registration efforts, it is also applicable to the QS-9000 registration process.

CONCLUSION

In most situations, QS-9000 registration is perceived as just one more project that must be squeezed in between current programs and activities. Obviously, a company cannot neglect the activities that keep the business running while working on QS-9000 registration. However, adequate preparation and organization are essential to QS-9000 registration in order to avoid unnecessary delays and frustration.

6

QUALITY AUDIT
FOR QS-9000
REGISTRATION

A quality audit may be defined as a documented activity performed in accordance with written procedures or checklists to verify, by examination and evaluation of objective evidence (not opinion), that a quality assurance system has been developed, documented, and effectively implemented to meet specific quality requirements. ISO 10011-1, -2, and -3 are the three *Guidelines for Auditing Quality Systems*. They are respectively entitled: (1) *Auditing*, (2) *Qualification Criteria for Quality Systems Auditors*, and (3) *Management of Audit Programs*. ISO 10011-1 defines a quality audit as: *"A systematic and independent examination to determine whether quality activities and related results comply with planned arrangements and whether these arrangements are implemented effectively and are suitable to achieve objectives."*

THE PURPOSE AND TYPES OF QUALITY AUDITS

Quality audits have been used by companies and government agencies to evaluate their own quality performance. This is commonly known as a *first-party* or *internal audit*. An audit used to assess the performance of a supplier is known as *second-party audit*. A second-party audit can reinforce the customer–supplier partnership by providing an excellent opportunity for both parties to get to know each other. Second-party audits, also known as *supplier quality assurance audits,* are either product or system audits. The purpose of such audits is to determine whether or not the supplier is in conformance with some prespecified contractual procedure imposed by the buyer/customer. When nonconformities are found, the burden of proof or the responsibility for corrective action lies with the auditee. Quality audits should never be intended to be punitive; rather, they should be conducted in a spirit of cooperation. Moreover, audits should not just be used to find out whether a quality system is meeting a predetermined set of standards; they should also allow for continuous improvement. Many supplier audits are designed not only to ensure conformance to quality requirements but also to promote a spirit of partnership. A quality audit attempts to evaluate the effectiveness of a quality assurance system and not the quality of a product.

With the current trend toward *just-in-time* (JIT) purchasing and inventory management, companies are increasingly focusing on quality of incoming inventories. With the development of a global marketplace for parts, subassemblies, and finished products, it is to the advantage of a supplier to have its quality system audited by an independent (other than its own or that of its buyers) auditor and certified under the ISO 9000/QS-9000 standards. An audit by an independent auditor for ISO 9000/QS-9000 registration or to meet any other standard (such as military, etc.) is commonly known as a *third-party audit*. A second- or third-party audit can provide independent assurance that a supplier: (1) plans to attain quality as required by the standards and specifications; (2) has developed a quality manual, procedures, and work instructions; (3) has installed and implemented (as well as committed resources for implementation and training) a quality assurance system; (4) has been keeping quality records (discrepancies and corrective actions, etc.); (5) has been following laws and regulations; and (6) has been striving for continuous improvement.

A quality system audit refers to the audit of a quality assurance system and not the audit of the quality of a product (known as a product audit). While a product audit involves the re-inspection of a product to verify the adequacy of acceptance and rejection decisions made by inspection and test personnel, a quality system audit (known as a systems audit) includes all activities that can affect the quality of the products manufactured by a company. A quality system audit addresses the quality aspects of various subsystems of an organization that independently or jointly affect the quality of its products. QS-9000 refers to all those subsystems that must be audited for full compliance. Therefore, a quality system audit reviews any or all of the subsystems referred to in QS-9000 over the whole range of products. Naturally, a systems audit is more time consuming than a product audit. Although the time spent in auditing a product or a system depends on the complexity of the product and the size of the organization, most audits last from two to five days. Third-party audits based on the QS-9000 series of standards are generally systems audits carried out by independent ISO-certified quality auditors assigned by a QS-9000-qualified registrar. (Contrary to the ISO registration process, the registrar must also be approved by the customer [big three automakers] in the QS-9000 registration process.)

THIRD-PARTY QUALITY AUDITS FOR QS-9000 REGISTRATION

Contrary to a second-party audit, where the burden of proof lies with the auditee, a third-party (independent) audit lays the burden of proof regarding nonconformities on the auditors. Therefore, before identifying a nonconformance, the auditor must find objective evidence (such as observations, measurement or test results, statements of facts, audit records, etc.) that proves the nonconformance and should not rely on opinion or subjective judgment.

The Third-Party Audit Process

ISO 10011-1 and 10011-2 generally set the guidelines for the third-party audit process. The process may, however, vary slightly from registrar to registrar. The client company generally makes the decision as to which quality system elements, physical locations, and organizational activities will be subjected to a third-party audit within a specified period of time. These decisions are made in consultation with the lead auditor. The client must provide sufficient objective evidence to demonstrate that its quality system functions effectively. Assessment of the effectiveness of the quality system is the primary objective of a third-party audit. Table 6.1 provides a list of activities involved in the third-party audit process.

TABLE 6.1 List of Activities in the Third-Party Audit Process

1. Preparation for audit
2. Pre-audit visit of the client by the lead auditor
3. Documentation review by the lead auditor
4. Audit planning by the lead auditor
5. Notification about the audit plan by the lead auditor
6. Pre-audit conference by the lead auditor with his or her team
7. The audit team conducts the audit
8. Post-audit conference between auditors and the auditee
9. Submission of the audit report to the client
10. Review of the report by the client's management
11. Corrective actions
12. Follow-up audit
13. Registration
14. Surveillance audit

Preparation for Audit

This step involves identifying which quality system elements, physical locations, product lines, or organizational activities will be audited. The client then sends all necessary documentation (such as contractual requirements, regulatory requirements, quality manual, procedures, work instructions, etc.) to the lead auditor of the registrar. The lead auditor examines all these documents and determines whether they meet the requirements of the standards.

He or she also conveys this assessment of these documents to the client and asks the client to correct any discrepancies. If the lead auditor needs any clarification or additional documentation, this is also conveyed to the client at this time.

Pre-Audit Visit to Client Facility by the Lead Auditor

Next, the lead auditor makes an appointment (no surprise visits) for a pre-assessment visit to the client's facility. During this visit, the lead auditor meets the client's management. The purpose of the pre-audit visit is manyfold. The visit allows the lead auditor to get to know the client and familiarize himself or herself with the site location in order to determine how many man-days will be required and what expertise the audit team will need on the day of the audit. The lead auditor also confirms the audit criteria and scope with the auditee's management. He or she also ascertains the product and regulatory requirements, discusses the assessment activities and the client's responsibilities, and tries to build a greater understanding with the client. The pre-assessment visit also helps the lead auditor determine the client's readiness for QS-9000 registration.

Documentation Review by the Lead Auditor

The lead auditor reviews all required documentation (such as the quality manual, procedures, work instructions, etc.) to determine whether they conform to the requirements of the pertinent QS-9000 standards.

Audit Planning by the Lead Auditor

The lead auditor selects his or her audit team and, with the assistance of the team, prepares the audit plan. This plan assigns audit activities to each member of the audit team (who will audit what). According to Section 5.2.1 of ISO 10011-1, the audit plan should be approved by the client and communicated to the auditors and auditee. The lead auditor should also develop a time frame for auditing and establish a mutually agreed upon date and time for the pre-audit conference.

Notification of the Audit Plan to the Client by the Lead Auditor

The lead auditor sends to the client a tentative agenda for all audit activities at least two weeks in advance and formally introduces his or her audit team members (enclose each auditor's resume). At the same time, the lead auditor should request escorts, accommodations, and meals for himself or herself and the team and ask the client's quality/management personnel, including the CEO, to attend the opening and closing meetings. According to ISO 10011-1, the client (auditee) has the right to review each auditor's credentials and then accept or reject anyone.

Pre-Audit Conference with Audit Team Members

At the pre-audit conference, the lead auditor personally introduces each audit team member, identifies each member's responsibilities, describes specific areas or procedures to be audited, sets guidelines for the audit, requests copies of necessary documents for reference, and schedules team meetings and debriefing meetings with the auditee personnel. He or she also explains how situations will be handled in case anything goes wrong. At the same time, the lead auditor tentatively schedules a post-audit conference with the auditee. Table 6.2 provides a typical agenda for a pre-audit conference.

Actual Audit

During the actual audit, the lead auditor makes sure that his or her team members are performing their assigned activities. He or she meets daily with the team members to discuss their experiences and observations. He or she also meets with the auditee's representative, according to a previously agreed upon schedule, for debriefings to report good findings as well as nonconformities. If nonconformities are found, the auditor must turn in evidence (observations) to the lead auditor. Regarding the observation of nonconformities, Section 5.3.2.1 of ISO 10011-1 strongly suggests that *"Evidence should be collected through interviews, examination of*

TABLE 6.2 Typical Agenda for a Pre-Audit Conference

8:00 A.M.	Team briefing
8:30 A.M.	Opening meeting
	Summary of the program
	Review the scope of the audit and the auditee's responsibilities
	Brief description of possible outcomes in unusual situations
	1. Recommendations for how to cope with them
	2. When to defer any decision
	3. When to terminate the audit
	Arrangements (time and place) for the post-audit conference with the auditee
9:00 A.M.	Start audit

documents, and observations of activities and conditions in the areas of concern. Clues suggesting nonconformities should be noted if they seem significant, even though not covered by checklists, and should be investigated. Information gathered through interviews should be tested by acquiring the same information from other independent sources, such as physical observation, measurements and records." The lead auditor always keeps the auditee fully aware of what is being observed during the actual audit period on a daily basis. He or she also confirms with the auditee the time and date of the post-audit conference.

Post-Audit Conference

At the post-audit conference, the lead auditor reports the results of the audit, including the list of conformities and nonconformities and objective evidence and tries to get the auditee management's to commit to taking specific corrective actions within a mutually agreed upon period of time. Sometimes the lead auditor tries to get a sign-off (confirmation) of the discrepancies and nonconformities from the auditee for his or her records.

Submitting Formal Audit Report

After gathering all information from the audit team members, the lead auditor prepares the formal audit report. It must include: (1) the scope of the audit, (2) participants' names and date of the audit, (3) list of nonconformities along with the QS-9000 reference, (4) the team's assessment of the client's quality system, and (5) a distribution list.

Review of the Formal Report by Client Management

The client management then reviews the formal audit report thoroughly. There is no need to panic if nonconformities are found. However, the auditee must provide a mutually agreed upon corrective action plan.

Submitting Corrective Action Plan by Auditee

If the audit report raises any nonconformity, the auditee must submit, within about thirty days, a mutually agreed upon corrective action plan and implement it accordingly. If more time is needed, this can be negotiated with the lead auditor. When all corrective actions have been addressed, the lead auditor determines whether or not another visit will be necessary. The lead auditor evaluates the effectiveness of the corrective actions, determines whether the deficiencies have been corrected, and informs the client of his or her evaluation.

Follow-Up Audit

The lead auditor may revisit the client for a follow-up audit to verify that the corrective actions are effective. If they are not satisfactory, the lead auditor may issue more corrective action requests and schedule additional audits.

Recommendation for Registration

Once satisfied, the lead auditor will send to the registrar his or her recommendation for the client's QS-9000 registration. Once recommended, it takes about sixty days to receive a certificate of registration from the registrar with the appropriate stamps. This registration certificate is generally valid for three years, at which time it must be renewed.

Surveillance Audit

The quality system is periodically revisited by the lead auditor to assure that the system is not degrading. The frequency of these visits or surveillance depends upon the registrar. In most cases, it is just a partial audit every six months and a complete audit every three years, when the registration certificate must be renewed. If serious nonconformities are found during surveillance, the registration certification may be revoked by the registrar.

THIRD-PARTY AUDITORS FOR QS-9000 REGISTRATION

After passing a standardized lead assessor training course, meeting educational and training requirements, and conducting at least five audits, a third-party auditor is certified and registered as a Quality System Auditor (QSA) by the Registrar Accreditation Board of the American Society for Quality Control in Milwaukee, Wisconsin or an International Quality Assessor (IQA) by the International Register of Certified Auditors of the Institute of Quality Assurance of London, U.K., or other ISO registrar. Unfortunately, despite certification, training, and experience, not all auditors interpret the standards identically. Some auditors are flexible and understand how to interpret the generic nature of the QS-9000 requirements, while others rigidly interpret every subsection. The auditor's background and experience must also be considered when selecting a team of auditors.

Qualifications for Quality System Auditors

The registrar and the regulatory body which accredits the registrar generally determine the qualifications and training requirements of a third-party auditor. ISO 10011-2 provides the following guidelines.

Language skill—The auditor must demonstrate fluency in the agreed upon language of the audit.

Personal attributes—Maturity, sound judgment, analytical skills, open-mindedness, tenacity, and an ability to understand complex operations from a broad perspective are some of the attributes called for by the standard.

Education—The auditor should have completed at least a secondary school education and should have demonstrated competence in clearly and fluently expressing concepts and ideas orally and in writing in his or her officially recognized language. Therefore, a high school diploma is a must, but many registrars require a bachelor's degree in arts, science, or engineering.

Training—The auditor should have received training to the extent necessary to ensure his or her competence in carrying out and managing audits. Such training may be accomplished by attending a five-day course recognized by the Registrar Accreditation Board (RAB) of the American Society for Quality Control (ASQC), the Institute of Quality Assurance (IQA) of London, or some other accreditation body. These courses are currently offered throughout the United States.

Experience—The standard requires a minimum of four years of experience in quality auditing, in addition to other requirements.

Management capabilities—The auditor must be able to demonstrate his or her ability to perform an audit (e.g., plan the audit, document observations, communicate and clarify audit requirements, report audit results, etc.) as specified in ISO 10011-1.

Competence upgrading—The auditor must continuously update his or her knowledge of and skill in conducting an audit.

A lead auditor must possess all of the above qualifications and in addition must have served as a qualified auditor in at least three audits performed in accordance with the recommendations stated in ISO 10011-1. The ISO 10011-1 requirements are just a generic model. Beyond these requirements, most registrars require their auditors to participate in at least five audits before being recognized as an auditor and five more before being given the title of lead auditor. National registration schemes usually append additional requirements to this ISO 10011-1 requirement. The National Accreditation Council for Certification Bodies (NACCB) of the U.K.'s IQA, for example, uses a scoring system to evaluate qualifications and experience. The RAB of the ASQC modeled its requirements on the NACCB and ISO guidelines. The RAB requires auditors to have a total of ten years of experience inclusive of training.

QS-9000 QUALITY SYSTEM ASSESSMENT PROCESS

Appendix A of *Quality System Requirements: QS-9000* (page 75) describes the quality system assessment process for the supplier's quality system. It provides the supplier with two choices of methods to verify conformance to QS-9000: (1) second-party (customer) audit and (2) third-party audit by a quality system registrar. However, the choice between these two options depends upon a number of factors, such as customer requirements, savings as a result of replacing multiple second-party (customer) audits with a third-party audit by a registrar, availability of a third-party registrar, and perceived value of third-party registration. A certificate citing conformance to QS-9000 must be obtained before the date(s) specified by the customer. Otherwise, the customer may review the supplier's tier one (quality manual) and tier two (quality procedures) documents, require the supplier to perform a self-assessment using *Quality System Assessment (QSA),* and examine the internal audit results and corrective action plans.

The customer may require the supplier to provide a copy of the certificate citing conformance to QS-9000 by an accredited third-party registrar, along with the reports. If the supplier has not yet received QS-9000 registration, then the customer may request the supplier to provide a plan, including a timetable, showing the supplier's process to achieve conformance with QS-9000 by third-party registration. The customer may also choose to perform on-site audits of its suppliers based upon the above and other information, such as whether or not the quality of products and services provided is satisfactory, whether the scope of QS-9000 registration is appropriate for the products or services provided, and so on. Generally, suppliers that have attained QS-9000 registration using a third-party registrar and whose products or services surpass customer quality requirements are not likely candidates for additional audits by the customer. However, additional audits by the customer have no bearing on QS-9000 registration, nor are they recognized by other customers.

CONCLUSION

The auditee must recognize that the registrar's objective is to verify that the quality system is in conformance with the requirements of QS-9000. If the quality assurance system is found not to be in conformance, the lead auditor will point out what needs to be done in order to bring the system in compliance with the standards. The process is more informative than punitive. Statistics shows that an average of 70% of all companies that have gone as far as their first ISO-9000 audit have achieved ISO-9000 registration. Because QS-9000 was introduced very recently (September 1994), only a few companies have received QS-9000 registration to establish any statistics. Because of the similarity of the processes, however, QS-9000 registration efforts may have the same or a better rate of success as ISO 9000 registration. Still, one of the best ways to evaluate the chance of success in a third-party audit for QS-9000 registration is to conduct a thorough internal audit in accordance with QS-9000 quality system requirements.

7

INTERNAL AUDIT FOR QS-9000 IMPLEMENTATION

QS-9000 Section 4.17 requires that the supplier establish a planned and documented system for an internal quality audit. Moreover, Section 4.1.2.2 of QS-9000 also specifies that the supplier identify in-house verification requirements, provide adequate resources, and assign trained personnel for verification activities. To ensure compliance with the standard, a company must establish an internal quality assurance function which must be independent of the production function in its organization. The total internal audit system must be documented, planned, scheduled, and conducted to assure coverage of all aspects of the quality system. It should also provide coordination of quality assurance activities. The internal audit system should be periodically reviewed and revised, if necessary, to ensure that the coverage and the schedule reflect current requirements and activities.

ESSENTIAL ELEMENTS OF AN EFFECTIVE INTERNAL AUDIT SYSTEM

In order to maintain the effectiveness of an internal audit system, the following essential elements must be included:

- Top management's commitment to an internal quality audit system

- A management policy statement or procedure which ensures the organizational independence and authority of the internal quality audit system

- Top management's commitment of adequate resources (manpower, facilities, and funding) to implement the internal quality audit system

- Identification of the personnel who will be responsible for the internal quality audit system and assignment of their authority, responsibilities, and organizational interdependence

- Provisions for timely and reasonable access of the quality assurance personnel to facilities, documents, and personnel in order to perform quality assurance activities

- Provisions for reporting the effectiveness of the quality audit system to the management of the auditee and the auditing organization

- Provisions for access of the audit personnel to all levels of management of the auditee and the auditing organization having responsibility and authority for taking corrective actions

- Provisions for verification of corrective actions on a timely basis

SCHEDULING INTERNAL QUALITY AUDIT ACTIVITIES

A plan for an internal quality audit must be prepared over a period of twenty-four months with scheduled audit activities. Table 7.1 provides an example of a typical twenty-four-month schedule

TABLE 7.1 A Typical Twenty-Four-Month Schedule of Audit Activities

Audit Area	Year 1												Year 2											
	J	F	M	A	M	J	J	A	S	O	N	D	J	F	M	A	M	J	J	A	S	O	N	D
Contract Rev.	X												X											
Design		X												X										
Manufacturing			X												X									
Receiving Insp.				X												X								
Process Insp.					X												X							
Final Insp.					X												X							
Testing						X												X						
Laboratories						X												X						
Purchasing							X												X					
Material Hand.								X												X				
Document Cont.									X												X			
Warehouses										X												X		
Quality Cont.											X												X	
Servicing												X												X

of audit activities for a hypothetical organization. Auditing must be initiated as early as possible to ensure effective quality assurance during the design, procurement, and contracting activities. All scheduled audits must be performed regularly in order to assure adequacy and conformance with the quality assurance system. Regularly scheduled audits must be performed on the basis of the status and importance of the activities. All applicable elements must be audited at least once a year or at least once in the lifetime of an activity, whichever is shorter.

THE INTERNAL AUDIT TEAM

Internal quality audit team members (auditors or assessors, a term commonly used for quality auditors) are chosen for auditing assignment based upon their education, personal characteristics, technical training, specialized training in auditing, and pertinent audit experience. A quality auditor must have conceptual, analytical, diagnostic, and synthesizing skills, as well as superior oral and written communication skills. A quality auditor should be able to offer advice on a professional basis in identifying, analyzing, and solving specific quality problems involving the design, planning, and control of activities. A quality auditor must serve as an impartial and objective observer using a certain set of quality standards as required by the customer (whether government or industry). An auditor may be a technical specialist in the area to be audited. Similarly, a management representative may also be a member of the audit team because of his or her expertise in management systems. The auditors selected must have the training or experience to develop their competence in performing the required audit activities. Particularly for auditing activities in accordance with QS-9000 requirements, auditors must have knowledge and understanding of the QS-9000 quality system requirements and must have received specialized training in auditing in accordance with the QS-9000 standards.

Since there is no such thing as a QS-9000-certified quality auditor, ISO-certified auditors with experience in auditing in automotive industries are the best candidates for a QS-9000 audit team. ISO quality auditor training and certification may be obtained by successfully completing a five-day lead assessor course offered by an officially approved agency and meeting the other criteria required by the registrar. A supplier must have a few of its internal auditors certified. Large companies may invite a consulting agency to offer an in-house auditor training course for their quality verification personnel. It is important that the five-day lead assessor course is approved by a registrar such as the Institute of Quality Assurance (IQA) of London or the Registrar Accreditation Board (RAB) of the American Society for Quality Control (ASQC). The advantage of attending an approved course is that the content is more or less standardized and it satisfies the partial requirement of ISO auditor certification. In order to become a registered auditor, it is also necessary to pass a two-hour exam. However, passing the exam does not automatically qualify you as a registered auditor. Participation in at least five audits (each registrar may have its own set of rules) under the supervision of a registered lead auditor is also required.

After conducting the required number of audits, an application may be submitted to the registrar, with the necessary fees for registration. After registration, the auditor's name is included in an official register of the registrar and he or she is considered an "official" ISO-9000-certified auditor (currently no such registration as a "QS-9000 auditor" is available). However, it is very difficult to get started with the first five audits. The only way to accomplish this is to start working for one of the registrars. An auditor is not generally allowed to conduct ISO/QS-9000 audits independently on his or her own. In the United States, the RAB has its own auditor certification procedures. The RAB in the United States and the IQA in the United Kingdom operate independently of each other. One may be officially trained as an (internal) auditor, but in order to become a fully accredited ISO/QS-9000 auditor, one must be associated with one of the registrars.

THE TEAM LEADER (LEAD ASSESSOR)

When the quality audit team consists of only one auditor, the auditor must be the lead assessor. When the team consists of more than one auditor, one must be designated the team leader or lead assessor. The lead assessor must be trained to organize and direct a quality audit, prepare the audit report, and evaluate corrective actions. The lead assessor should possess leadership qualities and have adequate knowledge of the industry to be audited. Above all, the lead auditor should have the ability to adjust rapidly to changing situations and work under tremendous pressure. Typically, a lead assessor will have a technical degree, a number of years of experience in the same line of business as the auditee, and a considerable amount of quality auditing experience.

The team leader is generally responsible for managing all phases of the audit. He or she generally selects the team members, represents the team, prepares the audit plan, makes all final decisions about the relevance of audit observations, and prepares and submits the final audit report. The lead auditor also orients the audit team, coordinates the audit process, conducts pre-assessment and post-assessment conferences, and evaluates corrective action plans. The team leader also provides each team member with the audit plan, the procedures, and the audit checklists as necessary to ensure that all audit activities are successfully accomplished.

DEVELOPING CHECKLISTS OF ITEMS TO BE AUDITED

Part of the preparation for conducting an internal audit of a quality system involves developing detailed checklists showing what items to audit, what questions to ask, who to ask, and the criteria or standards showing specific customer requirements based upon which the answers or observations should be evaluated. The checklist is a valuable tool for auditing. It saves valuable auditing time and can be used for multiple audits. With a checklist, an auditor is less likely to miss important items since he or she does not have to rely on his or her memory when developing questions during the audit. It also allows the auditor to review the questions and modify them as necessary based upon previous experience. In addition, the checklist allows the auditor to determine in advance the type of skill or expertise needed to evaluate responses to questions and the methods of evaluation (such as sample size, etc.) for audit analysis. The questions are generally placed in checklists in logical order to allow the audit to proceed smoothly.

There are many types of checklists, depending upon the specific requirements. Checklists also vary from company to company. A typical checklist for a quality assurance audit is provided in Table 7.2. In this checklist "organization" refers to the company being audited, and "audit subject" is the area being audited. "Department audited" is generally cited for internal auditing. "Audited by" refers to the auditor, and "person contacted" indicates who was contacted to obtain the information. "Requirements" are

TABLE 7.2 Typical Checklist for a Quality Assurance Audit

QUALITY ASSURANCE AUDIT							
ORGANIZATION: ABC Manufacturing Company Page 1 of 1							
Audit Subject: Inspection & Test Status							
Department Audited: Inspection							
Audited By: Jay Morgan							
Person Contacted: Jay Budd **Date**: 1/5/96							
No. **Revision**:							
REQUIREMENTS				**REQUIREMENT REFERENCE**			
Inspection & test status identified by using marking tags				4.12			
VERIFICATION METHODS							
Check 6 items at random							
FINDINGS				**STATUS**			
No tags used				Corrective action requested			
FOLLOW-UP ACTION							
Appropriate tags are being used now							
No.	Date	Reference	Originator	Status	By	Remark	
1005	1/5/96	K 40 /96	Jay Norris	Current	John Drake	O.K.	

the specific requirements with reference to the standards. "Verification methods" indicates how the situation will be verified with facts or observations. "Findings" are the actual observations made by the auditor. "Status" indicates whether or not the requirements were met. "Follow-up action" indicates whether corrective actions are being taken. Table 7.3 presents a slightly different checklist designed for a QS-9000 quality assurance audit.

REVIEW OF QUALITY ASSURANCE DOCUMENTS

A thorough study of all available and applicable quality assurance documents is essential to internal auditing. Table 7.4 lists all documents to be thoroughly examined in accordance with the standards and specified requirements. The auditor must review the quality assurance manual to make sure that it clearly specifies the quality objectives and quality policies of the organization in accordance with the QS-9000 standards and any other customer requirements. It should also demonstrate, using an organized approach, that the organization has established a documented operating quality system which translates the QS-9000 requirements into practices. It should also provide a documented means of measuring compliance and effectiveness of the quality assurance system. The auditor must find out when the quality system was originally implemented, whether the system is effective, provisions for revisions, whether it has been revised, provisions for documentation of such revisions, and whether the documentation is readily accessible.

The auditor should also study the organization chart, administrative procedures, quality assurance procedures, operating procedures, and work instructions. The organization chart must denote the lines of authority and responsibilities of assigned personnel, lines of communication, and interrelationships between the auditee's organization and its supporting facilities. Personnel responsible for checking, inspecting, verifying, and auditing must be clearly identified; their location in the organization must be specified; their degree of freedom in discharging their duties must be discussed; and the level of authority delegated to others must be mentioned. The auditor must also examine how the system is

TABLE 7.3 Checklist for an ISO 9001 Quality Assurance Audit

Quality Assurance Registration Program			NI	AD	UN	NC	NA	Inspection & Test Status	
ISO Section	Audit	Program Requirements						Verification Methods	Findings/ Comments
4.12	10	Inspection and test status identified by using marking tags						Check 6 items at random	O.K.
Number	Date	Originator	Status			Revision		Date	Remarks
1002	1/4/93	Jay Norris	Current			5th		1/5/96	

NI = needs improvement, AD = adequate, UN = unnecessary, NC = no change, NA = not applicable.

TABLE 7.4   List of Documents to Be Examined

• Quality assurance manual	• Corrective action reports
• Organization chart with personnel assignments	• Final product audit procedures
• Administrative procedures	• Material handling and storage procedures
• Quality assurance procedures	• List of machinery, equipment, and facilities
• Operating procedures	
• Work instructions	• Purchase orders
• Failure reports	• Engineering releases

continuously verified, corrected, and kept effective in terms of the auditee's organization, its suppliers, and other organizations in cases where the auditee has delegated the job of implementing a part of its quality assurance activities. The qualifications for quality assurance managers must be specifically described, and the auditor must examine whether or not these requirements have actually been implemented.

Other documents, such as material handling and storage procedures, final product audit procedures, failure reports, and corrective action reports, must be examined for their clarity, effectiveness, and practicality. Design and engineering release documents and change notices must also be reviewed to make sure that they contain specific information, approval signatures by the appropriate authorities, and a distribution list in order to disseminate the information through appropriate channels to the persons affected by the changes.

CONDUCTING THE AUDIT

During the audit, a planned sequence of events is followed in order to ensure that the quality assurance activities are reviewed, analyzed, and evaluated according to the audit plan. These events include:

1. Auditors use checklists as a guide. Checklists should not restrict the audit investigation. When a nonconformance is found, further questions are raised.

2. Only objective evidence is examined for compliance with the requirements of standards.

3. Only selected elements are audited to the degree necessary to determine whether they are being implemented effectively.

4. When a system deficiency or nonconformance is found through the audit, the root cause of the problem must be identified and the necessary corrective action options evaluated and determined.

5. System deficiencies or nonconformances must be acknowledged by a member of the auditee's organization.

6. If a condition requires immediate corrective action, it must be reported immediately to the management of the audited organization.

7. Attention must be given to corrective actions on any nonconformances identified during the previous audit.

During an audit, the auditee must not be put on the defensive. The audit should be a constructive activity for the betterment of all concerned. Findings must be based upon objective evidence and documented properly. When an opinion is expressed, it should be stated as such. The auditor should always get the manager of the audited organization to acknowledge any deficiency detected. Courtesy and firmness are key to the success of an auditor's approach. An auditor should be polite and patient, but should be firm in getting the details, without being sidetracked by evasive answers or voluminous irrelevancies. After recording documentation samples related to an audit question, the auditor should follow through with on-site/in-person verification of the activities shown in the paperwork. It is critical that the persons involved, and not just the supervisor, be asked questions. The lowest level of personnel should be involved in questioning.

Auditing uses sampling techniques. Auditors should not be satisfied with document samples provided by the auditee. Auditors should select samples on their own. If the verification method requires ten samples, then ten samples should be selected. If ten samples are not available, the situation should be noted or an explanation given.

AUDITING TECHNIQUES

Although checklists with written questions provide a general idea of the subjects which need to be covered, those questions are seldom asked verbatim. The auditor should ask questions in such a way as to solicit meaningful and useful answers from the auditee. The following are some helpful auditing techniques which may be used by the auditor:

- Try to get the answers to questions through observations or facts.

- When asking a question, ask why, when, how, who, and what.

- When necessary, go beyond the scope of the written questions and ask for greater detail.

- To uncover problems, if necessary, ask several different people the same question.

- Ask the person directly involved, instead of the boss or staff.

- Verify and evaluate all findings. Use phrases such as "show me" to solicit evidence.

- Obtain copies of local practices instead of company plans. This provides an opportunity to evaluate local practices.

- Inform the auditee that you will be taking notes in order to maintain accurate records.

- Try not to be critical of a violation. Let the auditee know about the specific code or requirement that is being violated.

- Recommend concepts only, and not plans or corrective actions

- Avoid making recommendations off the top of your head without having the facts.

- Never attack personalities; instead, point out the weakness of the job.

- Never make any comment, especially a negative comment, about other organizations by name.

- Show sincerity and professionalism. Make the auditee feel that you are there to do a job.

- Do not reveal your opinion about an answer through facial expressions or comments.

- Learn as much as possible from your audience.

- Keep promises, but make as few promises as possible.

- Always be a good listener, and compliment the auditee.

- Demonstrate a proper attitude, observe business ethics, and be professional.

- Try to maintain control of the interview. Keep questions short and to the point.

- Write the summary results promptly after the audit is completed

An auditor should not be sarcastic and should avoid attacking personalities. He or she must not argue with people or criticize employees in front of the boss. The auditor should not be late for or drink before the interview and should not use profanity. The auditor should not discuss politics or company policy, must not use the names of other companies he or she has audited, and should not allow disagreement among team members during the interview. The auditor should also avoid "yes or no" questions and should not ask questions beyond his or her level of knowledge. Finally, the auditor should never make the audit too secretive.

ELEMENTS OF SUCCESSFUL INTERVIEWS

Most audits involve interviewing a number of people. An interview is essentially a method of collecting information, and it must be carried out in such a way that pertinent information is gathered. The following suggestions may be helpful in conducting an interview:

- Conduct the interview using a checklist or a plan.

- Keep the interview to the subject for which it was planned.

- Guide the interview with your questions.

- Listen and be sure that you understand what was said and meant. Cross-check facts with other individuals within the organization, if necessary.

- Evaluate the method and the results of the interview.

Before conducting an audit of an internal supplier/department, the auditor should try to obtain an organization chart of the department and a schematic diagram of the production process. The organization chart allows the auditor to plan the audit and estimate the time needed for interviews. A schematic process diagram can help formulate specific questions to be asked during the audit. Since it is impossible to remember exactly who said what and when, it is a good idea to carry a small notebook when visiting a plant or interviewing people. For each interview, the time of day and name of the person being interviewed must be noted. A tape recorder may be used, but the auditee must be informed that he or she is being recorded. At the end of each interview, the auditor should prepare a summary of what has been said. These in-between interview summaries are extremely valuable. They allow the auditor to summarize what has been said, which in turn allows him or her to modify or otherwise prepare for the next interview. They also provide the auditor with a much needed rest period between interviews, to avoid feeling rushed from one interview to the next. Effective listening is the key element in any good audit, but it is quite exhausting. Therefore, in order to stay effective, an auditor should schedule at least two pauses a day.

The auditee frequently perceives the auditor as a stranger who should not be trusted—someone who is wasting his or her precious time or someone who is looking for a fault in the system and who usually finds it. In order to avoid mistrust and doubt, the auditor should always clearly state the purpose of the audit, which should simply be to verify the effectiveness of the quality assurance system. If the system is ineffective, then corrective action may be requested. Punitive actions, negative and in particular destructive criticism, and sarcasm must be avoided.

THE ART OF QUESTIONING

A good question helps the auditee express himself or herself; stimulates thought; channels information; provokes a reaction; explores, clarifies, and verifies facts; and allows the auditee to answer freely. Questions should be designed to collect facts and not opinions, feelings, or vague concepts. Phrases such as "in principle" and "in theory" should be restated as "in reality" and "in practice," respectively. Questions may be designed as closed or open-ended. A closed question leads to a very precise answer, such as yes or no, and tends to discourage any dialogue. An open-ended question allows for greater flexibility. An example of an open-ended question would be: "Tell me more about your calibration procedure." Questions may also be designed to obtain clarification, such as, "Could you give me an example of..." The auditor should avoid implying his or her opinion by using questions like "Don't you think that..." It is often helpful for the auditor to repeat the answer(s) just heard to confirm his or her understanding with the auditee. This is known as the mirror effect.

From the point of view of the auditee, questions can be perceived as a form of intrusion. Every time a question is asked, it is advisable to impose a frame of reference within which the auditee must try to answer to the best of his or her ability. It is not wise to rush through the interview, ask too many questions at the same time, or ask too lengthy questions. Unless the auditor is interviewing a particular department, he or she should first meet the plant manager and his or her staff, which would include the quality manager or the nearest equivalent. The purpose of the visit should be explained. The auditor may start with the receiving department, go through purchasing, the lab, quality assurance, production scheduling, maintenance, packaging, etc., and finish with the shipping department. On the other hand, the auditor may also follow the reverse path. In either case, the auditor must be looking for documented evidence instead of opinions.

An interview may take anywhere from fifteen to forty-five minutes. Before terminating an interview, the auditor must give the respondent one last chance to mention anything which he or she thinks is significant but has not been mentioned. The auditor must also get the respondent's commitment to review the interview report. For a three-day audit, an auditor may expect to spend an average of eight hours interviewing people, about four hours checking documentation, and another eight hours touring the plant and/or talking to operators. Only the last four hours is devoted to the important debriefing meeting with the auditee.

SUGGESTIONS FOR HANDLING DIFFICULT INTERVIEW SITUATIONS

The following suggestions may be helpful when handling difficult interview situations:

- If it appears that the respondent does not know the answer or is trying to guess, the auditor must double check the answer given after the interview.

- If the respondent starts giving irrelevant information or telling stories, the auditor must tactfully attempt to get the discussion back on track.

- If the respondent stops talking as soon as the interviewer starts taking notes, the auditor should stop taking notes.

- If the respondent seems to resent the interviewer and appears to be withholding data, the auditor should try to ease the situation by talking about something of interest to the respondent.

- If the respondent attempts to sabotage the interview, the auditor should ask if someone else can provide the information.

- If the respondent complains about his or her job or unfair treatment from the supervisor, the auditor should listen sympathetically.

- If the respondent expresses great satisfaction with the way things are currently done, the auditor must encourage him or her to elaborate about how things are done to find out if fact or opinion is being stated.

THE QUALITY AUDIT REPORT

After the post-audit conference, the team leader is responsible for preparing the final audit report. The final audit report is a written record of findings, analyses, conclusions, and agreements on corrective actions. The final audit report should include:

- A description of the scope of the audit

- Identification of the auditors

- A list of the persons interviewed during pre-audit, audit, and post-audit activities

- A summary of the audit results, specifically evaluating the effectiveness of the quality system elements which have been audited

- A description of all deficiencies in sufficient detail so that corrective actions can be effectively implemented

- The auditee's plan for corrective actions, with a date specifying when and by whom each corrective action will be completed

- When appropriate, pertinent quotations collected by the auditors during their visit in order make a point

If a questionnaire was used during the audit, the scored questionnaire must be returned. For a supplier quality assurance audit, the auditor may conclude his or her report by offering suggestions for how both parties can resolve any problems (whereas for a third-party audit, the auditor must never suggest any solutions to problems). Records of all quality audits must be maintained, and the audit process itself must be reviewed periodically by top management.

GETTING READY FOR AN AUDIT

A certain amount of preparation may be helpful in getting ready for an audit. The auditee must start preparing well in advance (about three to four weeks) of the actual date of the audit. Because some internal auditors prefer to conduct their audits unannounced, it is important to be prepared. If possible, the questionnaire or audit procedures that will be used should be requested from the lead auditor. The auditee should study these items as part of the preparation. It is often a good idea to rehearse an audit. It is advisable to have the pre-audit conducted by an outside (independent) auditor. This will guarantee objectivity and allows the auditee to focus on the audit activities.

When the auditors arrive, it is unwise to hide any weaknesses. This may encourage the auditors to dig even deeper. It is also unwise to volunteer information not requested by the auditors. Answers should be short and to the point. All pertinent documentation must be ready and accessible for examination by the auditors.

Although it is a good idea to escort the auditors in order to control the audit as much as possible, the auditee must demonstrate confidence in his or her organization by allowing the auditors the freedom to explore whenever and wherever they want and interview whomever they please.

CONCLUSION

Internal auditing is an important activity that allows departments to continuously improve how they function. It is an essential requirement of QS-9000. Trained internal auditors can provide valuable assistance and advice in preparing for QS-9000 registration. Unfortunately, internal audits often are not taken seriously, which a third-party auditor may interpret as a sign of limited managerial commitment. In many situations, internal auditors are perceived as policemen or enforcers of the QS-9000 quality assurance system.

Many department heads wrongly assume that it is the responsibility of the internal auditor to address all corrective actions. The function of the internal auditor is to point out deficiencies within the system and not to address corrective actions. Since the auditors are not directly responsible for the department being audited, they should not be expected to correct the deficiencies they pointed out. The deficiencies should be corrected by the noncompliant department. Thus, by understanding the role and function of internal auditing, an organization can continuously improve its quality assurance system. Finally, the internal audit function can help monitor the quality assurance system and achieve readiness for QS-9000 registration.

8

REGISTRARS FOR ACCREDITATION

Once a quality assurance system has been documented and implemented, an accredited registrar must be consulted for QS-9000 registration. Selection of the appropriate registrar is as critical as the process of registration. When selecting a registrar, it is important to recognize that although any registrar can issue a certificate, *not all certificates are recognized by all customers.* Consequently, care must be exercised when selecting a registrar. It is important to find out in which countries a registrar's certificate will be valid. This depends upon the original accreditation agency. For example, a company that exports to the United Kingdom should look for a registrar accredited by the National Accreditation Council for Certification Bodies (NACCB) of England, which issues a certificate with the Crown Stamp of the NACCB. Only a NACCB-accredited registrar can issue the certificate. The NACCB publishes its own *Directory of Accredited Certification Bodies.* This should not be confused with the directory entitled *Association of Certification Bodies* published by the British Standards Institution, which lists all accredited and nonaccredited certification bodies.

U.S. REGISTRARS

On December 13, 1991, a National Program for Quality Registrar Accreditation was launched jointly by the American National Standards Institute (ANSI) and the American Society for Quality Control's (ASQC) Registrar Accreditation Board (RAB). This joint program is known as the American National Accreditation Program for Registrars of Quality Systems. ANSI coordinates the joint program's due process procedures and provides the program with national recognition and international acceptance. The RAB's accreditation is based on ISO/QS-9000 guidelines. The entire system of registration of supplier companies and accreditation of registrars is based upon auditing. Because there was no system in the United States for certifying auditors, in February 1992 the RAB developed the Certification Program for Auditors of Quality Systems, based upon the internationally accepted standard ISO 10011. The RAB also provides a nationally recognized program for accrediting registrars of quality systems according to the European Norm (EN) 45000 series of standards, which govern all conformity assessment activities. In order to gain international recognition, the RAB incorporates all the criteria of EN 45012, which is the basic document used by the European Community. It is important to recognize that a registrar is an organization which utilizes accredited auditors to conduct a third-party audit of an organization that applies for registration. The auditors conduct the audit, but registration is granted or denied by the registrar based upon the report of the auditors.

ACCREDITATION OF A REGISTRAR BY THE RAB

The following steps are commonly used by the RAB in accrediting a registrar:

- The prospective organization files an application to become a registrar.
- The RAB reviews the preliminary information provided by the applicant and checks for conflicts of interest and other problems.

- RAB auditors evaluate two tiers of documentation used by the applicant organization: tier one—the quality manual and tier two—procedures.

- RAB auditors then evaluate the applicant organization against the RAB criteria for accreditation and request corrective actions if necessary.

- The RAB audit team visits the prospective registrar's site and audits its actual performance against what was presented in the written documentation and against the RAB criteria.

- RAB auditors accompany the prospective registrar's auditors on an on-site visitation of a supplier company in order to actually observe the complete audit process from start to the end of the closing meeting.

- The RAB audit team submits a report of the results of the audit and its recommendation.

- Based upon the report of the RAB auditors, the Accreditation Council of the RAB decides whether to grant or deny accreditation to the registrar.

- Upon approval, the RAB accredits the registrar by issuing a certificate. This allows the registrar the right to use the RAB's mark in addition to its own mark on its letterhead and in advertisements. These marks cannot be used on any product.

A current list of organizations approved as accredited registrars can be obtained from their accrediting agencies upon request. A partial list of registrars currently operating in the United States is provided in Appendix D.

EUROPEAN REGISTRARS

A common perception is that a company can only be registered to the ISO/QS-9000 requirements either by a British registrar, an associate of a British registrar, or a registrar accredited by the NACCB of the United Kingdom. However, this is not necessarily true. Although the U.K.'s Institute of Quality Assurance (IQA) and the NACCB have taken the lead in organizing and implementing a sound accreditation program, it should not be assumed that the British accreditation scheme is the sole legitimate program in Europe.

In Germany, Traegergemeinschaft fuer Akkreditierung GmbH (TAG) is the accrediting body for all registrars. Similarly, in the Netherlands, Raad voor de Certificatie (RvC) is the accreditation authority for all registrars. It has also accredited many American (and foreign) registrars, such as Houston-based ABS Quality Evaluation, Inc. and Virginia-based Intertek. A list of accrediting bodies is provided in Appendix E.

It is important to note that some registrars are accredited by more than one accrediting body. Some foreign registrars currently operating in the United States are accredited by the U.K.'s NACCB and the Netherlands' RvC. Many registrars have been in existence for several decades and are recognized in a number of countries. Registrars in the United States can be categorized into two groups: (1) those accredited only by the RAB of Milwaukee and (2) those accredited by both the RAB and one or more accrediting body of other governments, such as the NACCB of the United Kingdom or RvC of the Netherlands.

WHICH REGISTRAR TO CHOOSE?

Before selecting an accredited registrar, a company must find out if its operation is within the scope of the registrar. The scope determines whether the registrar has the required competence/knowledge of the industry in which a company is engaged. The NACCB and the IQA ensure that a registrar operating under their accreditation audits a particular industry only if the registrar has competency within that industry. The scope of each accredited registrar is listed in the *Directory of Accredited Certification Bodies*. In most cases, if competency cannot be found within its ranks, a registrar generally tries to contact a knowledgeable auditor by referring to a register of certified auditors. Currently, the demand for audits far exceeds the availability of auditors. Consequently, although a registrar will always have certified auditors perform an audit, it cannot always guarantee that the auditors will be the most knowledgeable in the particular industry being audited.

Of course, the NACCB's views are not shared equally by other accreditation agencies. The European Network for Quality System Assessment and Certification (EQNET) (a network of third-party certification bodies) considers four broad categories of competence or scope: hardware, software, processed materials, and service. The argument proposed by the EQNET is that in order to audit a quality system, it is not necessary to be competent in all aspects of the quality system. Accordingly, experts in the service industry should be allowed to audit any service industry. The ISO Technical Committee 176 subscribes to the same philosophy. It strongly believes that auditors should be accredited (certified) generically instead of on an industry or economic sector basis. Each audit team should include at least one person (auditor or expert) knowledgeable in the particular industry or economic sector(s) involved in the audit. Although each approach has its own rationale, each faces potential difficulties. Expert auditors sometimes forget that they are auditing a quality system; they occasionally have a tendency to revert back to their second-party role and offer advice and recommendations on how to best fix a problem rather than focus the system as a whole. Auditors with experience in one industry may have difficulty evaluating a quality system of an industry unfamiliar to them.

Finally, it is important to realize that the selection of a third-party registrar is not imposed by any customer. The selection process depends solely on a company's own criteria and concerns about certification issues. Therefore, a company should "shop" for a registrar and identify at least three candidates before making a selection.

QUALITY SYSTEM REGISTRAR FOR QS-9000

Appendix B: Code of Practice for Quality System Registrar (page 79) of *Quality System Requirements: QS-9000* contains twelve requirements for a QS-9000 registrar (for details, refer to the document). Any registrar that agrees to follow all twelve requirements in this code of practice is authorized to perform a third-party QS-9000 audit.

This code of practice requires that a QS-9000 registrar must be accredited by a customer-recognized national accreditation body (e.g., RAB, NACCB, RvC) and that the registrar's scope of accreditation include all products and services provided by the supplier to one or more of its customers subscribing to QS-9000. The registrar must conform to the current EN 45012: General Criteria for Certification Bodies Operating Quality Systems Certification and the accompanying guidelines. If an organization, or its subsidiaries or affiliates, provides consulting services to a particular client, the organization cannot be accepted as a registrar for that client and cannot supply the client with auditors for a third-party audit. Each member of the registrar's team performing a QS-9000 audit must have successfully completed Quality System Assessment (QSA) and QS-9000 training courses approved by the company issuing the QS-9000 certificate (evidenced by a certificate of completion issued by the appropriate authority).

The registrar assesses all elements of the supplier's quality system for effective implementation of QS-9000 requirements and their effective practice. This may go beyond QS-9000 to make sure that elements meet customer needs as evidenced by the results of at least one complete internal audit and management review cycle. Each on-site audit must include a review of: (1) customer complaints and responses, (2) internal audit and management review and corrective actions, and (3) evidence of continuous improvement.

The supplier's entire quality system must be audited once every three years and a surveillance audit conducted every six months. Each manufacturing location of the supplier must be individually audited and certified. A full report on the operation audited must be provided by the audit team to the supplier within forty-five days of each initial and surveillance audit. This report must follow Model B of the current publication entitled *Guidelines for Compiling Reports on Quality Systems Audits,* published by RvC. Opportunities for improvements are to be included in the report, without recommendations for specific solutions. The checklist used by the audit team must include, but is not limited to, all questions in the

QSA. If unresolved major or minor nonconformances exist, then the quality system will not be registered to QS-9000.

CONCLUSION

The selection of a registrar is, of course, a critical decision. Although most registrars operate very similarly, each has its own format for issuing nonconformances. Some issue minor and major nonconformances, while others use a point (rating) system. A company should select the registrar that best fits its business needs and corporate profile. Companies exporting to Canada may select Canadian registrars. Others may prefer non-American registrars because of their long-time expertise, overseas recognition, or simply because they export mostly to a particular country. Still others may select an American registrar. Before selecting any registrar, however, it is wise to contact more than one and ask as many questions as possible to find out who they are and how they operate. A supplier should review the Code of Practice with potential registrars during the negotiation stage. Only the registration certificate citing conformance to QS-9000 is acceptable by customers that subscribe to QS-9000. A supplier registered to ISO 9000 standards may consider including QS-9000 in its registration. In such cases, the supplier must contact its registrar, update its quality system documentation to meet QS-9000, and identify the updated documentation in the next surveillance visit. The registrar then verifies conformance with QS-9000 and issues a certificate of registration.

BIBLIOGRAPHY

Arter, Dennis R., *Quality Audits for Improved Performance*, ASQC, Milwaukee, Wisconsin, 1989.

Aubrey, C.A., and Felkins, P.K., *Teamwork: Involving People in Quality and Productivity Improvement*, Quality Resources, White Plains, New York, 1988.

Automotive Industry Action Group (AIAG), *Measurement Systems Analysis: Reference Manual*, Automotive Industry Action Group, Southfield, Michigan, 1990.

_____ , *Fundamental Statistical Process Control: Reference Manual*, Automotive Industry Action Group, Southfield, Michigan, 1991.

_____ , *Potential Failure Mode and Effects Analysis*, Automotive Industry Action Group, Southfield, Michigan, 1993.

_____ , *Production Part Approval Process*, Automotive Industry Action Group, Southfield, Michigan, 1993.

_____ , *Advanced Product Quality Planning and Control Plan: Reference Manual*, Automotive Industry Action Group, Southfield, Michigan, 1994.

_____ , *Quality System Assessment*, Automotive Industry Action Group, Southfield, Michigan, 1994.

_____ , *Quality System Assessment Training*, Automotive Industry Action Group, Southfield, Michigan, 1994.

_____ , *Quality System Requirements: QS-9000*, Automotive Industry Action Group, Southfield, Michigan, 1994.

Bandyopadhyay, J.K., *ISO 9000 Series of Quality Standards: How to Achieve Compliance and Registration*, Quality & Productivity International, Midland, Michigan, 1993.

_____ , "Quality Key to Improve Productivity," *International Journal of Management*, June 1993, pp. 264–269.

_____ , "POKA YOKAY Systems to Insure Zero Defect Quality in Manufacturing," *International Journal of Management*, March 1993, pp. 29–33.

Block, M.R., "ISO/TC 207: Developing an International Environmental Management Standard," *European Marketing Guide*, March 1994, pp. 12–14.

Bobbit, C.E. Jr., "Conduct More Effective Audits," *Quality Progress*, October 1993, pp. 60–63.

Bodinson, G.W., "Warning: Ignoring ISO Standards May Be Harmful to Your Company's Future," *Industrial Management*, March/April 1991, pp. 11–12.

Boehling, W.H., "Europe 1992: Its Effect on International Standards," *Quality Progress*, June 1990, pp. 29–32.

Bounds, G.M., *Cases in Quality*, Richard D. Irwin, Homewood, Illinois, 1995.

British Standards Institution (BSI), *BS 7750: Environmental Management Systems*, British Standards Institution, London, United Kingdom, 1992.

Bureau of Business Practice, *Profile of ISO 9000*, Allyn and Bacon, Needham Heights, Massachusetts, 1992.

Burrows. P., "Behind Facade of ISO 9000," *Electronic Business*, January 27, 1992.

Burstein, Daniel, *Euroquake*, Simon & Schuster, New York, 1991.

Byrnes, D.J., "ISO 9000 Style Eco-audits," *PI Quality*, November/December 1993, pp. 3–7.

Chauvel, A.M., "Quality in Europe: Towards the Year 2000," *Quality Management Journal*, January 1994, pp. 71–77.

Chrysler Corporation, *Packaging and Shipping Instructions Manual*, Chrysler Supplier Quality Office, Auburn Hills, Michigan, 1990.

_____ , *Shipping/Parts Identification Label Standards Manual*, Chrysler Supplier Quality Office, Auburn Hills, Michigan, 1990.

Clements, R., Sidor, S.M., and Winters, R.E. Jr., *Preparing Your Company for QS-9000*, ASQC Quality Press, Milwaukee, Wisconsin, 1995.

Coleman, J., "Qualifying a Quality Success," *Quality*, October 1994, pp. 4–5.

Cook, N.P., "Quality System, Poor Products?" *ISO 9000 News*, July/August 1993, pp. 2–5.

Dertouzos, Michael L., Lester, Richard K., and Solow, Robert M., *Made in America*, Harper Perennial, MIT Press, Cambridge, Massachusetts, 1990.

Durant, A.C., and Durant, I., "The Role of ISO 9000 Standards in Continuous Improvement," *Quality Systems Update*, October 1993, pp. 19–24.

Durant, I., McRobert, C., Middleton, D., and Tirato, J., "Document and Data Control Requirements of the ISO 9000 Series Standard," *Quality Systems Update*, May 1992, pp. 32–34.

Dusharme, D., "ISO 9000 Certification Costs," *Quality Digest*, January 1995, p. 8.

Dzus, G., "Planning a Successful ISO 9000 Assessment," *Quality Progress*, November 1991, pp. 43–46.

Dzus, G., and Sykes, E.G. Sr., "How to Survive ISO 9000 Surveillance," *Quality Progress*, October 1993, pp. 58–62.

Eade, T., and Byrnes, D.J., "Documentation per ISO 9000," *PI Quality*, September/October 1993, pp. 2–3.

Earnshaw, D., "The EC's Eco-Management and Audit Scheme," *EC Marketing Guide*, November 1993, pp. 16–17.

Eckstein, A.L., and Balakrishnan, J., "The ISO Series: Quality Management Systems for the Global Economy," *Production and Inventory Management Journal*, Fourth Quarter, 1993.

Egan, L., "Software Configuration Management," *Continuous Improvement*, November 1993, pp. 1–4.

Finlay, J. S., "ISO 9000, Malcolm Baldrige Award Guidelines and Deming/SPC-Based TQM—A Comparison," *Quality Systems Update*, August 1992, pp. 1–9.

Ford Motor Company, *Planning for Quality*, Ford Motor Company, Total Quality Excellence and Systems Management, Corporate Quality Office, Dearborn, Michigan, 1990.

_____ , *Ford Instructional Systems Design Process,* Ford Motor Company, Instructional Methods Section, Dearborn, Michigan, 1992.

_____ , *Failure Mode and Effects Analysis: Handbook,* Ford Motor Company, Engineering Materials and Standards, Technical Affairs, Dearborn, Michigan, 1993.

_____ , *QOS Assessment & Rating Procedure,* Ford Motor Company, Quality Publication Department, Farmington Hills, Michigan, 1993.

_____ , *Acronym List,* Ford Motor Company, Supplier Quality Engineering: NAAO Vehicle Operations, Dearborn, Michigan, 1994.

_____ , *Quality Operating System,* Ford Motor Company, Supplier Quality Engineering, Dearborn, Michigan, 1994.

Frame, J.D., *The New Project Management,* Jossey-Bass, San Francisco, California, 1994.

Garavaglia, P.L., "How to Insure Transfer of Training," *Training and Development,* October 1993, pp. 65–68.

Gladis, S.D., "Are You the Write Type?" *Training and Development,* July 1993, pp. 46–48.

Goult, R., "ISO: Implementing an ISO 9000 Series," *Quality Systems Update,* January–May 1992, pp. 12–14.

Graham, J.P., "Texas Petrochemical Plant Gets Certification," *The Oil & Gas Journal,* May 13, 1991, pp. 10–12.

Greeno, J.L., Hedstrom, G.S., and DiBerto, M., *Environmental Auditing: Fundamentals and Techniques* (2nd edition), Center for Environmental Assurance, Arthur D. Little, Inc., Cambridge, Massachusetts, 1995.

Grounds, R., "Employee Involvement: A Major Change in Direction," *Quality Digest,* October 1993, pp. 30–32.

Guzzetta, S., "How ISO 9000 Changed Supplier Quality Assurance," *PI Quality,* September/October 1993, pp. 3–4.

Harrington, H.J., *Poor-Quality Cost,* ASQC, Milwaukee, Wisconsin, 1987.

Hayes, R.H., and Wheelwright, S.C., *Restoring Our Competitive Edge: Competing Through Manufacturing,* John Wiley & Sons, New York, 1984.

Haynes, M.E., *Project Management: Four Steps to Success,* Crisp Publications, Los Altos, California, 1989.

Horovitz, J., and Cudennec-Poon, C., "Putting Service Quality into Gear," *Quality Progress*, January 1991, pp. 54–58.

Hovermale, R.A., "ISO 9000—Continual Improvement," *European Marketing Guide*, February 1994, pp. 23–25.

Howe, K.R., and Dougherty, K.C., "Ethics, Institutional Review Boards, and the Changing Face of Educational Research," *Educational Researcher*, December 1993, pp. 12–15.

International Standard ISO 10011-1 1990-12-15, *Guidelines for Auditing Quality Systems—Part 1: Auditing*, Geneva, Switzerland, 1987.

International Standard ISO 10011-2 1991-05-01, *Guidelines for Auditing Quality Systems—Part 2: Qualification Criteria for Quality Systems Auditors*, Geneva, Switzerland, 1987.

International Standard ISO 10011-3 1991-05-01, *Guidelines for Auditing Quality Systems—Part 3: Management of Audit Programmes*, Geneva, Switzerland, 1987.

Jeffrey, N., "Minimizing and Disposing of Hazardous Waste Requires More than Lip Service," *American Printer*, January 1994, pp. 56–61.

Jones, L., and McBride, R., *An Introduction to Team Approach Problem Solving*, ASQC Quality Press, Milwaukee, Wisconsin, 1990.

Juran, J.M., and Gryna, F.M., *Quality Planning and Analysis* (2nd edition), McGraw-Hill, New York, 1980.

Kacker, R.N., "Quality Planning for the Service Industries," *Quality Progress*, August 1988, pp. 39–42.

Kalinosky, I.S., "The Total Quality System—Going Beyond ISO 9000," *Quality Progress*, June 1990, pp. 50–54.

Kaufman, R., and English, F.W., *Needs Assessment*, Educational Technology Publications, Englewood Cliffs, New Jersey, 1979.

Kerzner, H., *Project Management: A Systems Approach to Planning, Scheduling and Controlling* (5th edition), Van Nostrand Reinhold, New York, 1995.

King, C.A., "A Framework for a Service Quality Assurance System," *Quality Progress*, September 1987, pp. 27–32.

Kinni, T.B., "Preparing for Fast-Track ISO 9000 Registration," *Quality Digest*, October 1993, pp. 16–19.

_____, "Reengineering Primer," *Quality Digest*, January 1994, pp. 26–31.

Kochan, A., "ISO 9000: Creating a Global Standardization Process," *Quality*, October 1993, pp. 4–5.

Kolka, J.W., "ISO 9000 and EC Medical Devices," *EC Report on Industry*, November 1993, pp. 14–15.

_____, "EN 46000 and the EU Medical Devices," *The European Report on Industry*, March 1994, pp. 13–17.

_____, "EU General Product Safety Directive," *The European Marketing Guide*, June 1994, pp. 12–13.

_____, "Product Design, Product Software and Product Liability," *European Marketing Guide*, March 1994, pp. 25–27.

_____, "Registration to ISO 9000 Grows Worldwide," *On Q*, April 1994, p. 4.

Kromrey, J.D., "Ethics and Data Analysis," *Educational Researcher*, May 1993, pp. 3–5.

Lamprecht, J.L., "ISO 9000: Strategies for the 1990s," *Quality Magazine*, November 1991, pp. 79–88.

_____, "The ISO Certification Process: Some Important Issues to Consider," *Quality Digest*, August 1991, pp. 75–85.

_____, "Demystifying the ISO 9000 Series Standards, *Quality Engineering*, Vol. IV, No. 2, 1992, pp. 45–51.

Landrum, R., "12 Reasons to Implement ISO 9000," *Quality Digest*, December 1993, pp. 12–16.

LeDoux, T.J., "ISO 9000: What You Don't Know Might Hurt You," *Continuous Journey*, December/January 1993–94, pp. 6–8.

Lofgren, G., "Quality Systems Registration." *Quality Progress*, May 1991, pp. 35–37.

Mar, W., "Seven Keys to Better Project Teams," *Quality Digest*, October 1993, pp. 21–23.

Marash, I.R., "ISO 9000 and the Medical Device GMP," *European Report on Industry*, February 1994, pp. 7–9.

Marquardt, D. et al., "Vision 2000: The Strategy for the ISO 9000 Series Standards in the 90's," *Quality Progress*, May 1991, pp. 25–31.

_____, "ISO 9000: A Universal Standard of Quality," *Management Review*, January 1992, pp. 50–52.

Martin, J., *Supplier Communication: Bulletin No. 94Nt98*, General Motors Corporation NAO, Detroit, Michigan, October 1994.

Mclntosh, B., "European Community Legislation on Machinery," *EC Report on Industry*, November 1993, pp. 16–19.

Meeker, W.Q., and Hahn, G.J., *How to Plan an Accelerated Life Test*, ASQC Quality Press, Milwaukee, Wisconsin, 1985.

Michael, N., and Burton, C., *Basic Project Management*, Institute of Management, Singapore, 1993.

Mills, Charles A., *The Quality Audit: A Management Evaluation Tool*, ASQC, Milwaukee, Wisconsin, 1989.

Morrow, David J., "Be Good Or," *International Business*, July 1991, pp. 24–28.

Moura, E.C., *How to Determine Sample Size and Estimate Failure Rate in Life Testing*, ASQC Quality Press, Milwaukee, Wisconsin, 1991.

Nisbett, John and Aburdene, Patricia, *Megatrends 2000. Ten New Directions For the 1990's*, Avon Books, New York, 1990.

Opper, S., and Fersko-Weiss, H., *Technology for Teams*, Van Nostrand Reinhold, New York, 1992.

Paton, S.M., "The Baldrige, the Deming, ISO 9000 and You," *Quality Digest*, August 1991, pp. 18–26.

Petrick, K., "ISO 9000 and the Environment—Competing Interests," *European Report on Industry*, February 1994, pp. 21–23.

Porter, Michael E., *The Competitive Advantage of Nations*, Free Press, New York, 1990.

Rabbit, J.T., Bergh, P.A., and Dror, Y., "Capture a Quality Image with ISO 9000," *INTECH Applying Technology*, April 1993, pp. 5–6.

Ramsay, M., "ISO 9000: The Myths and Misconceptions," *APICS: The Performance Advantage*, June 1992, pp. 55–57.

Raymond, C., "An Afternoon with an Admiral," *OEM Off-Highway*, November 1993, pp. 40–42.

Remich, Norman C. Jr., "Europe 1992 a Plus for Some Appliance Makers," *Appliance Manufacturer*, May 1990, pp. 64–66.

Robinson, Charles B., *How to Plan an Audit*, ASQC, Milwaukee, Wisconsin, 1987.

Sayle, Allan J., *Management Audits: The Assessment of Quality Management Systems* (2nd edition), ASQC, Milwaukee, Wisconsin, 1988.

Schindler, G., and Lamprecht, J.L., "The Significance of the International Standards Organization ISO 9000 Series for the Drilling and Production Related Businesses," *The Oil and Gas Journal*, May 1991, pp. 40–42.

Schleffler, S., "What Is World-Class, Mature Quality?" *Continuous Journey*, August/September 1993, pp. 12–13.

Scholtes, P.R., *The Team Handbook*, Joiner Associates, Madison, Wisconsin, 1988.

Shonk, J.S., *Team-Based Organizations: Developing a Successful Team Environment*, Business One Irwin, Homewood, Illinois, 1992.

Silver, C.H. Jr., "Is Your Company Being Torn Apart by Teamwork?" *OEM Off-Highway*, November 1993, pp. 16–20.

Skrabec, Q.R. Jr., "Integrating Quality Control into Your TQM Process," *Quality Digest*, January 1994, pp. 66–70.

Sloan, D., and Weiss, S., *Supplier Improvement Process Handbook*, ASQC, Milwaukee, Wisconsin, 1987.

Society for Automobile Engineers, *Potential Failure Mode and Effects Analysis in Design and Potential Failure Mode and Effects Analysis in Manufacturing and Assembly Processes: Process Manual*, Society for Automobile Engineers, Michigan, 1994.

Stamatis, D.H., "FMEA Fulfills Prevention Intent of ISO 9000," *Quality Systems Update*, September 1993, pp. 15–17.

_____ , *Failure Mode and Effect Analysis: FMEA from Theory to Execution*, ASQC Quality Press, Milwaukee, Wisconsin, 1995.

_____ , *Integrating QS-9000 with Your Automotive Quality System*, ASQC Quality Press, Milwaukee, Wisconsin, 1995.

_____ , "ISO 9000 and BS 7750," *Environmental Journal*, March 1995, pp. 15–21.

Stamatis, D.H., Epstein, I., and Cooney. R.P., "Documenting Personnel Qualifications," *Quality Systems Update*, June 1993, pp. 21–23.

Stout, G., "Quality Practices in Europe," *Quality*, October 1993, pp. 6–7.

Talley, Dorsey J., *Management Audits for Excellence*, ASQC, Milwaukee, Wisconsin, 1988.

Teich, A.H., *Technology and the Future*, St. Martin's Press, New York, 1993.

Wayman, W.R., "ISO 9001: A Guide to Effective Design Reviews," *Quality Digest*, January 1994, pp. 45–48.

Wellins, R.S., Byham, W.C., and Wilson, J.M., *Empowered Teams*, Jossey-Bass, San Francisco, California, 1991.

Willborn, Walter, *Audit Standards: A Comparative Analysis*, ASQC, Milwaukee, Wisconsin, 1987.

_____ , *Quality Management System: A Planning and Auditing Guide*, ASQC, Milwaukee, Wisconsin, 1989.

Wolak, J., "ISO 9000—A Software Market," *Quality*, March 1994, pp. 64–65.

APPENDIX A

SUGGESTED FORMAT FOR A QUALITY ASSURANCE MANUAL

There are various ways to write a quality assurance manual. Because a registrar may prefer a particular format, checking with the registrar before starting to prepare your quality manual may save a lot of time. The following two formats are commonly used in writing quality assurance manuals.

FORMAT 1

Many quality manuals are written by dividing a section or subsection into five distinct paragraphs:

1.0 **Purpose:** Why was this section written?

2.0 **Scope:** What activities need to be controlled?

3.0 **Description/procedures:** How are they controlled?

4.0 **Responsibilities and authority:** Who is responsible?

5.0 **Reference:** Which documents are referred to in this section?

FORMAT 2

Many other manuals use a condensed and informal format which briefly describes:

1.0 How the QS-9000 section or subsection is covered in the organization

2.0 The authority and responsibilities of the functions or individuals involved in carrying out the activities covered under the section or subsection

3.0 Names of documents to be referred to, if any

Format 2 has been used in preparing the quality assurance manual presented below.

NAME OF THE COMPANY

Location of the Plant
Address & Telephone No.

QUALITY ASSURANCE MANUAL

Control Copy No.

Developed and Issued By

Date of Initial Issue

Revision No.
Date of Revision

Logo	**QUALITY ASSURANCE MANUAL**	Page of

SECTION	SUBJECT	EFFECTIVE DATE	REVISION
0.0	Foreword	July 7, 1995	1.0

FOREWORD

A brief foreword to the manual is provided by the president of the company.

Example

The most important goal of _____ Corporation is to design and manufacture parts and subassemblies of consistent quality and reliability and deliver them to its customers on time. The company has been continuously attempting to improve the quality of its products and delivery performance in order to both satisfy the needs of its customers and generate customer enthusiasm. The purpose of this quality manual is to establish the authority and responsibilities of the quality function as it relates to the other functions in the organization in order to achieve compliance with QS-9000 quality system requirements and to guide the quality assurance system. The principles and guidelines established in this quality manual are applicable to all management functions of the organization. Each manager is responsible for coordinating the development and implementation of the quality assurance programs that directly concern and affect him or her.

This manual has been issued and controlled by _____ _____ on behalf of the organization.

_____   _____

Signed by   Dated

President, _____ Corporation

Approved by:	Issued by:
Signature:	Signature:
Approval Date:	Issue Date:
Revision:	Revision Date:

Logo	**QUALITY ASSURANCE MANUAL**		Page of
SECTION	*SUBJECT*	*EFFECTIVE DATE*	*REVISION*
	Table of Contents	July 7, 1995	1.0

TABLE OF CONTENTS
Example

Element	Description	Revision	Date	Page
0.0	**Foreword**			
1.0	**Revisions**			
2.0	**Distribution list**			
3.0	**Introduction**			
3.1	Manual control policy			
4.0	**SECTION I: ISO-based requirements**			
4.1	**Management responsibility**			
4.1.1	Quality policy			
4.1.2	Organization			
4.1.2.1	Responsibility and authority			
4.1.2.2	Verification resources and personnel			
4.1.2.3	Management representative			
4.1.3	Management review			
4.1.4	Business plan			
4.1.5	Analysis and use of company-level data			
4.1.6	Customer satisfaction			

Approved by:	**Issued by:**
Signature:	**Signature:**
Approval Date:	**Issue Date:**
Revision:	**Revision Date:**

Logo	**QUALITY ASSURANCE MANUAL**		Page	of

SECTION	SUBJECT	EFFECTIVE DATE	REVISION
	Table of Contents (contd)	July 7, 1995	1.0

Approved by:	**Issued by:**
Signature:	**Signature:**
Approval Date:	**Issue Date:**
Revision:	**Revision Date:**

Logo	**QUALITY ASSURANCE MANUAL**	Page	of

SECTION	SUBJECT	EFFECTIVE DATE	REVISION
	Table of Contents (contd)	July 7, 1995	1.0

Approved by:	Issued by:
Signature:	Signature:
Approval Date:	Issue Date:
Revision:	Revision Date:

Logo	**QUALITY ASSURANCE MANUAL**		Page of
SECTION	*SUBJECT*	*EFFECTIVE DATE*	*REVISION*
	Table of Contents (contd)	July 7, 1995	1.0

Approved by:	**Issued by:**
Signature:	**Signature:**
Approval Date:	**Issue Date:**
Revision:	**Revision Date:**

Logo	**QUALITY ASSURANCE MANUAL**	Page of

SECTION	*SUBJECT*	*EFFECTIVE DATE*	*REVISION*
	Table of Contents (contd)	July 7, 1995	1.0

Element	*Description*	*Revision*	*Date*	*Page*
4.15	**Handling, storage, packaging, preservation, and delivery**			
4.15.1	General			
4.15.2	Handling			
4.15.3	Storage			
4.15.4	Packaging			
4.15.5	Preservation			
4.15.6	Delivery			
4.16	**Control of quality records**			
4.17	**Internal quality audits**			
4.18	**Training**			
4.19	**Servicing**			
4.20	**Statistical techniques**			
4.20.1	Identification of Need			
4.20.2	Procedures			
5.0	**SECTION II: Sector-specific requirements**			
5.1	**Production part approval process**			
5.1.1	General			
5.1.2	Engineering change validation			
5.2	**Continuous improvement**			
5.2.1	General			

Approved by:	**Issued by:**
Signature:	**Signature:**
Approval Date:	**Issue Date:**
Revision:	**Revision Date:**

Logo	**QUALITY ASSURANCE MANUAL**		Page of
SECTION	*SUBJECT*	*EFFECTIVE DATE*	*REVISION*
	Table of Contents (contd)	July 7, 1995	1.0

Element	*Description*	*Revision*	*Date*	*Page*
5.2.2	Quality and productivity improvements			
5.2.3	Techniques for continuous improvement			
5.3	**Manufacturing capabilities**			
5.3.1	Facilities, equipment, process planning, and effectiveness			
5.3.2	Mistake-proofing			
5.3.3	Tool design and fabrication			
5.3.4	Tooling management			
6.0	**SECTION III: Customer-specific requirements**			
	Chrysler-specific requirements (for Chrysler suppliers only)			
6.1	**Parts identified with symbols**			
6.2	**Significant characteristics**			
6.3	**Annual layout**			
6.4	**Internal quality audits**			
6.5	**Design validation/product verification**			
6.6	**Corrective action plan**			
6.7	**Packaging, shipping, and labeling**			
6.8	**Process sign-off**			

Approved by:	**Issued by:**
Signature:	**Signature:**
Approval Date:	**Issue Date:**
Revision:	**Revision Date:**

Logo	**QUALITY ASSURANCE MANUAL**	Page of

SECTION	SUBJECT	EFFECTIVE DATE	REVISION
	Table of Contents (contd)	July 7, 1995	1.0

Element	Description	Revision	Date	Page
	Ford-specific requirements (for Ford suppliers only)			
6.1	Control item parts			
6.2	Critical characteristics			
6.3	Set-up verification			
6.4	Control item fasteners			
6.5	Heat treating			
6.6	Process changes and design changes for supplier-responsible designs			
6.7	Supplier modification of control item requirements			
6.8	Engineering specification test performance requirements			
6.9	System design specification			
6.10	Ongoing process monitoring			
6.11	Prototype part quality initiatives			
6.12	Quality operating system			

Approved by:	Issued by:
Signature:	Signature:
Approval Date:	Issue Date:
Revision:	Revision Date:

Logo	**QUALITY ASSURANCE MANUAL**		Page of

SECTION	*SUBJECT*	*EFFECTIVE DATE*	*REVISION*
	Table of Contents (contd)	July 7, 1995	1.0

Element	*Description*	*Revision*	*Date*	*Page*
	General Motors-specific requirements (for General Motor NAO suppliers only)			
6.1	**C4 technology program**			
6.2	**Key characteristics designation system**			
6.3	**Supplier submission of material for process approval**			
6.4	**Problem reporting and resolution**			
6.5	**Supplier submission of match check material**			
6.6	**Component verification and traceability**			
6.7	**Continuous improvement**			
6.8	**Evaluation and accreditation of supplier test facilities**			
6.9	**Early production containment**			
6.10	**Traceability identifier requirements**			
6.11	**Specifications for part and component bar codes**			
6.12	**Suppliers of material for prototype**			
6.13	**Packaging and identification for production parts**			
6.14	**Shipping/parts identification labeling**			
6.15	**Shipping and delivery performance**			
6.16	**Customer approval of control plans**			
6.17	**UPC labeling for commercial service parts**			

Approved by:	**Issued by:**
Signature:	**Signature:**
Approval Date:	**Issue Date:**
Revision:	**Revision Date:**

Logo	**QUALITY ASSURANCE MANUAL**		Page of
SECTION	*SUBJECT*	*EFFECTIVE DATE*	*REVISION*
1.0	Revisions	July 7, 1995	1.0

REVISIONS

Date	Page	Paragraph	Comments	Approval By

Approved by:	Issued by:
Signature:	Signature:
Approval Date:	Issue Date:
Revision:	Revision Date:

Logo	**QUALITY ASSURANCE MANUAL**	Page of

SECTION	SUBJECT	EFFECTIVE DATE	REVISION
2.0	Distribution List	July 7, 1995	1.0

2.0 Distribution List

Provide a distribution list stating who will receive a copy of this manual.

Example

All distributed control copies of the quality manual are issued and distributed to the following department heads by the quality assurance department.

Copy No.	Department	Personnel
1	Administrative Bldg.	President
2	Quality Assurance	Quality Assurance Director
3	Plant	Plant Manager
4	Laboratory	Chief Chemist
5	Maintenance	Maintenance Director
6	Human Resources	Human Resource Manager
7	_____	_____

Note: **Control copies of the manual must be identified clearly either by printing them on special paper and/or by using the company seal or stamp.** *The manual may be borrowed, reviewed, or otherwise photocopied by anyone and thus may not always reside permanently at said location. The person in charge of said department is responsible for the manual and its subsequent circulation.* **Photocopies of the manual are not considered to be control copies.**

Approved by:	Issued by:
Signature:	Signature:
Approval Date:	Issue Date:
Revision:	Revision Date:

Logo	**QUALITY ASSURANCE MANUAL**		Page of
SECTION	*SUBJECT*	*EFFECTIVE DATE*	*REVISION*
3.0	Introduction	July 7, 1995	1.0

3.0 Introduction

In this section, a brief description can be inserted to include the plant's history and products and corporate objectives. The section need not be more than a few paragraphs long. It is also a good idea to include a paragraph covering scope of services.

Example

In 1960, _____ Corporation was founded in _____ (town), _____ (state), _____ (country). The company is engaged in the design and manufacture of auto parts and sub-assemblies. It employs about _____ workers and is organized into _____ department units. The company has decided to achieve registration in compliance with QS-9000 quality system requirements. This quality manual defines the quality assurance system, establishes the authority for and responsibilities of the quality function as it relates to the other functions in order to achieve compliance with QS-9000 quality system requirements, and provides general procedures for all activities comprising the quality assurance system.

This manual is issued and controlled by the quality assurance function on behalf of the organization.

Approved by:	Issued by:
Signature:	Signature:
Approval Date:	Issue Date:
Revision:	Revision Date:

Logo	**QUALITY ASSURANCE MANUAL**		Page of
SECTION	*SUBJECT*	*EFFECTIVE DATE*	*REVISION*
3.1	Manual Control Policy	July 7, 1995	1.0

3.1 Manual Control Policy

Briefly describe how the content of and revisions to the manual should be controlled. Also describe which functions or individuals are responsible for control of the manual.

Example

1. Anyone may submit revisions to the quality manual, but all revisions must be approved by the plant manager.

2. The quality assurance manager must ensure that the latest version of the manual is distributed to all interested parties.

3. Prior to issuance of a new updated version, all obsolete copies of the quality manual must be first retrieved by the quality assurance manager.

4. Control copies of the quality manual must be printed on special company paper and identified by the company seal.

5. All revisions to the quality manual must be logged on the *Revision* page.

6. _____

   _____

7. _____

   _____

Approved by:	Issued by:
Signature:	Signature:
Approval Date:	Issue Date:
Revision:	Revision Date:

Logo	**QUALITY ASSURANCE MANUAL**	Page of

SECTION	*SUBJECT*	*EFFECTIVE DATE*	*REVISION*
4.1	Management Responsibility	July 7, 1995	1.0

4.1 Management Responsibility

Briefly describe the quality philosophy of top management and how top management has delegated the quality assurance responsibilities and authority within the organization.

Example

Total customer satisfaction and total quality management underlie the quality philosophy of the organization, with the goal of providing high-quality products to customers. The sole responsibility and authority for quality rest with the president. However, they are delegated to the director of quality assurance, who reports directly to the president.

Approved by:	**Issued by:**
Signature:	**Signature:**
Approval Date:	**Issue Date:**
Revision:	**Revision Date:**

Logo	**QUALITY ASSURANCE MANUAL**	Page of

SECTION	*SUBJECT*	*EFFECTIVE DATE*	*REVISION*
4.1	Management Responsibility (contd)	July 7, 1995	1.0

4.1.1 Quality Policy

Briefly describe the quality policy of the organization as laid down by top management.

Example

_____ Corporation's quality policy recognizes the importance of consistency in quality and reliability in manufacturing and servicing of its products not only in meeting customer requirements but also in achieving customer enthusiasm. This is accomplished by employee participation in the careful planning, design, manufacturing, and testing of products with the intent of continuous improvement of quality and customer satisfaction. This policy has been formulated by the president and approved by the board of directors.

_____

Signed by: President

This quality policy must be discussed with and explained to all existing and new employees in orientation meetings or training session. A log of such meetings or training sessions must be maintained. This quality policy must also be posted on bulletin boards at prominent locations across the company.

Approved by:	**Issued by:**
Signature:	**Signature:**
Approval Date:	**Issue Date:**
Revision:	**Revision Date:**

Logo	**QUALITY ASSURANCE MANUAL**	Page of

SECTION	*SUBJECT*	*EFFECTIVE DATE*	*REVISION*
4.1	Management Responsibility (contd)	July 7, 1995	1.0

4.1.2 Organization

Briefly describe the delegation of responsibility and authority in the organization and explain how the quality assurance program can be accomplished across all levels of the organization. Also provide an organization chart showing delegation of authority and responsibilities.

Example

The organization is designed in a way that allows organizational freedom in identifying, initiating, recommending, and implementing corrective action for any quality problem and verifying that the corrective action is properly implemented. The organization chart shows the responsibility and authority of each of the quality functions.

Approved by:	Issued by:
Signature:	Signature:
Approval Date:	Issue Date:
Revision:	Revision Date:

Logo	**QUALITY ASSURANCE MANUAL**	Page of

SECTION	SUBJECT	EFFECTIVE DATE	REVISION
4.1	Management Responsibility (contd)	July 7, 1995	1.0

4.1.2.1 Responsibility and Authority

Briefly describe the responsibility and authority of each function involved in quality assurance activities.

Example

1. The company president will regularly assess the status and adequacy of the quality assurance program.

2. The TQM steering committee is responsible for establishing the direction and leading the implementation of quality programs.

3. The quality assurance function is responsible for:

   a. All TQM training and consultations

   b. All QMS process management activities

   c. Annual quality planning process

   d. All quality analysis and reporting activities

   e. All SPC and QC activities

   f. All internal quality audit training and activities

   g. _____

A paragraph describing the responsibility of each major function within the organization must be included here. Following the QS-9000 format, the next step would be to address issues.

Approved by:	Issued by:
Signature:	Signature:
Approval Date:	Issue Date:
Revision:	Revision Date:

Logo	**QUALITY ASSURANCE MANUAL**	Page of

SECTION	SUBJECT	EFFECTIVE DATE	REVISION
4.1	Management Responsibility (contd)	July 7, 1995	1.0

4.1.2.2 Verification Resources and Personnel

Briefly describe how the company identifies its resource requirements and allocates necessary resources for managing, performing, and verifying quality-related activities, including internal auditing.

Example

The company has established the quality assurance department under the leadership of the quality assurance director, who reports directly to the president and is responsible for all quality-assurance-related activities across the company, including internal quality auditing.

There are three quality managers (one for each shift at the plant), three internal quality auditors, and fifteen quality technicians (five on each shift).

Approved by:	Issued by:
Signature:	Signature:
Approval Date:	Issue Date:
Revision:	Revision Date:

Logo	**QUALITY ASSURANCE MANUAL**		Page of
SECTION	*SUBJECT*	*EFFECTIVE DATE*	*REVISION*
4.1	Management Responsibility (contd)	July 7, 1995	1.0

4.1.2.3 Management Representative

Briefly define the authority and responsibilities of the management representative for ensuring that the company's quality system has been established, implemented, and maintained in accordance with QS-9000 standards.

Example

The company has appointed a QS-9000 coordinator who is responsible for establishing, implementing, and maintaining the quality assurance system of the company in accordance with the QS-9000 quality system requirements.

4.1.3 Management Review

Briefly describe how and how often the quality assurance system of the company is reviewed by the top management of the company and how the log of such reviews is maintained.

4.1.4 Business Plan

Briefly describe the short-term and long-term goals of the company, methods of determining current and future customer expectations, and the processes for collecting information. The company must prepare a formal business plan which must be mentioned here as a reference document.

Approved by:	Issued by:
Signature:	Signature:
Approval Date:	Issue Date:
Revision:	Revision Date:

Logo	**QUALITY ASSURANCE MANUAL**	Page of

SECTION	SUBJECT	EFFECTIVE DATE	REVISION
4.1	Management Responsibility (contd)	July 7, 1995	1.0

4.1.5 Analysis and Use of Company-Level Data

Briefly describe how the company documents quality-related data and determines quality trends, operational performance (effectiveness, efficiency, productivity), and current quality levels and compares them with those of its competitors and/or appropriate benchmarks.

4.1.6 Customer Satisfaction

Briefly describe an established documented procedure by which the company determines customer satisfaction objectively at periodic intervals. Also describe how trends in customer satisfaction are determined and how these trends are compared to those of competitors or benchmarks and reviewed by top management.

Approved by:	Issued by:
Signature:	Signature:
Approval Date:	Issue Date:
Revision:	Revision Date:

Logo	**QUALITY ASSURANCE MANUAL**		Page of
SECTION	*SUBJECT*	*EFFECTIVE DATE*	*REVISION*
4.2	Quality System	July 7, 1995	1.0

4.2.1 General

Briefly describe the quality system of the organization which is designed to accomplish compliance with QS-9000 quality system requirements.

Example

The quality system of _____ Corporation is designed to facilitate the corporate objective of being a world-class supplier of parts and subassemblies to the big three automakers. In keeping with this policy, the quality system is modeled after QS-9000 quality system requirements. This system provides a framework for clearly defining the control of materials, processes, and verification activities to assure that the design, manufacture, and servicing of products are performed to meet and exceed customers expectations.

4.2.2 Quality System Procedures

The company must document its operational procedures and place these documents in a file called Quality Assurance Procedures (QAP). Documented procedures may make reference to work instructions that explain how an activity is performed. Refer to the Quality Assurance Procedure Manual and briefly describe how these procedures and work instructions are effectively implemented. Discuss the complexity of the work, the methods used, and the skills and training requirements for performing the activities.

Approved by:	**Issued by:**
Signature:	**Signature:**
Approval Date:	**Issue Date:**
Revision:	**Revision Date:**

Logo	**QUALITY ASSURANCE MANUAL**		Page of
SECTION	*SUBJECT*	*EFFECTIVE DATE*	*REVISION*
4.2	Quality System (contd)	July 7, 1995	1.0

4.2.3 Quality Planning

The company must prepare quality plans (control plans) to define and document how quality requirements will be met with respect to its products, projects, or any contracts. The company should use the Advanced Product Quality Planning (APQP) and Control Plan Reference Manual in preparing its quality plans. The company should also prepare failure mode and effects analysis (FMEA) for its products and identify processes with special characteristics, such as the Shield for safety and the Diamond for critical characteristics. Refer to these quality plans (control plans) and FMEAs and briefly describe how these plans are implemented effectively.

Approved by:	Issued by:
Signature:	Signature:
Approval Date:	Issue Date:
Revision:	Revision Date:

Logo	**QUALITY ASSURANCE MANUAL**	Page	of

SECTION	SUBJECT	EFFECTIVE DATE	REVISION
4.3	Contract Review	July 7, 1995	1.0

4.3.1 General

Confirm that the company has established and is maintaining documented procedures for contract review and coordination of such activities.

4.3.2 Contract Review

Briefly describe how contract reviews and related activities are performed and list the responsibilities and authority of the individuals involved in contract review.

Example

All contract reviews are performed by the contract review function at the corporate office. Contract specifications consist of a twenty-digit number which identifies several parameters, including customer code, specification, and other characteristics.

Production planning is organized by the engineering department, which is in direct contact with the corporate office and other departments via the company's computer network system.

Approved by:	Issued by:
Signature:	Signature:
Approval Date:	Issue Date:
Revision:	Revision Date:

Logo	**QUALITY ASSURANCE MANUAL**	Page of

SECTION	*SUBJECT*	*EFFECTIVE DATE*	*REVISION*
4.3	Contract Review (contd)	July 7, 1995	1.0

4.3.3 Amendment to a Contract

Briefly describe how an amendment to a contract is made.

4.3.4 Records of Contract Reviews

Briefly describe how the records of contract reviews are maintained. Also explain how channels of communication and interface with the customer have been established in connection with contract-related activities.

Approved by:	Issued by:
Signature:	Signature:
Approval Date:	Issue Date:
Revision:	Revision Date:

Logo	QUALITY ASSURANCE MANUAL		Page of
SECTION	SUBJECT	EFFECTIVE DATE	REVISION
4.4	Design Control	July 7, 1995	1.0

4.4.1 General

The company shall establish and maintain documented procedures for verifying and controlling design of products to customer specification. Briefly describe these documented procedures.

4.4.2 Design and Development Planning

Briefly describe how designs are developed, verified, validated, approved, recorded, released, and updated. Also describe the design and developmental planning processes and the production part approval process (PPAP). Also describe the responsibilities and authority of each individual/function associated with design development and control activities.

4.4.3 Organizational and Technical Interfaces

Define the organizational and technical interfaces between different groups that provide input to the design process. Also describe how the necessary information is documented, transmitted, and regularly reviewed.

4.4.4 Design Input

Briefly describe how design input requirements related to the product are identified, documented, and reviewed.

Approved by:	Issued by:
Signature:	Signature:
Approval Date:	Issue Date:
Revision:	Revision Date:

Logo	**QUALITY ASSURANCE MANUAL**	Page	of

SECTION	*SUBJECT*	*EFFECTIVE DATE*	*REVISION*
4.4	Design Control (contd)	July 7, 1995	1.0

4.4.5 Design Output

Briefly describe how design outputs are documented, verified, and validated against design input requirements, including those critical to the safe and proper functioning of the product.

4.4.6 Design Review

Briefly describe the formal documented review of the design results at appropriate stages of design.

4.4.7 Design Verification

Briefly describe the formal design verification process to ensure that design stage output meets the design stage input requirements.

4.4.8 Design Validation

Briefly describe the formal design validation process which follows the successful design verification process.

4.4.9 Design Changes

Briefly describe how all design changes and modifications are identified, documented, reviewed, and approved by authorized personnel before their implementation.

Approved by:	Issued by:
Signature:	Signature:
Approval Date:	Issue Date:
Revision:	Revision Date:

Logo	**QUALITY ASSURANCE MANUAL**	Page of

SECTION	*SUBJECT*	*EFFECTIVE DATE*	*REVISION*
4.5	Document & Data Control	July 7, 1995	1.0

4.5.1 General

Describe briefly how all documents and manuals belonging to corporate, divisional, and departmental levels are prepared, updated, distributed, and stored. Also describe the responsibilities and authority of the individuals/functions involved in document and data control activities.

4.5.2 Document and Data Approval and Issue

Briefly describe how documents are reviewed and approved by authorized personnel before they are issued. Prepare a master document list showing the current revision status of all documents.

4.5.3 Document and Data Changes

Describe briefly how document and data changes are reviewed and approved. Also describe the authority and responsibilities of the functions involved. Make sure that the same functions/organizations that performed the original review and approval also perform the review and approval of changes, unless otherwise designated.

Approved by:	**Issued by:**
Signature:	**Signature:**
Approval Date:	**Issue Date:**
Revision:	**Revision Date:**

Logo	**QUALITY ASSURANCE MANUAL**		Page of
SECTION	*SUBJECT*	*EFFECTIVE DATE*	*REVISION*
4.6	Purchasing	July 7, 1995	1.0

4.6.1 General

Briefly describe the established procedures to ensure that any purchased product conforms to specified requirements.

Example

A list of subcontractors approved by the customer is maintained. All relevant materials for ongoing production are procured from subcontractors on this list.

4.6.2 Evaluation of Subcontractors

Briefly describe how subcontractors are selected and controlled. Maintain a list of approved subcontractors. Also describe how quality records for acceptable subcontractors are maintained.

4.6.3 Purchasing Data

Briefly describe how purchasing documents have been designed to contain data clearly describing the product ordered, including all its applicable characteristics. Also describe the responsibilities and authority of the individuals/functions involved in related activities.

4.6.4 Verification of Purchased Product

Briefly describe how the company verifies its purchased or subcontracted products to ensure that they conform to specified requirements.

Approved by:	Issued by:
Signature:	Signature:
Approval Date:	Issue Date:
Revision:	Revision Date:

Logo	**QUALITY ASSURANCE MANUAL**	Page of

SECTION	SUBJECT	EFFECTIVE DATE	REVISION
4.7	Control of Customer-Supplied Product	July 7, 1995	1.0

4.7 Control of Customer-Supplied Product

Briefly describe how customer-supplied products are verified, stored, and incorporated into supplies. Also describe how any such products which are lost, damaged, or otherwise unsuitable for use will be recorded and reported to the customer. Also describe the responsibilities and authority of the individuals/functions involved in activities described in this section.

Example

Customer-owned components are received as a part of the repair and return program. Upon receipt of such materials, they are identified and separated from other returned parts. Each return is reviewed, repaired, and repackaged. A label is affixed to each package for identification and traceability.

Approved by:	Issued by:
Signature:	Signature:
Approval Date:	Issue Date:
Revision:	Revision Date:

Logo	**QUALITY ASSURANCE MANUAL**		Page of
SECTION	*SUBJECT*	*EFFECTIVE DATE*	*REVISION*
4.8	Product Identification and Traceability	July 7, 1995	1.0

4.8 Product Identification and Traceability

Briefly describe how all products are identified for traceability upon receipt and at all stages of production, delivery, and installation. Also describe the responsibilities and authority of the individuals/functions involved in activities described in this section.

Example

Upon receipt, all materials are identified and tagged. After inspection, components found to be defective are separated, tagged as rejects, and stored in designated storage areas until they are returned to their suppliers.

Approved by:	Issued by:
Signature:	Signature:
Approval Date:	Issue Date:
Revision:	Revision Date:

Logo	**QUALITY ASSURANCE MANUAL**	Page of

SECTION	SUBJECT	EFFECTIVE DATE	REVISION
4.9	Process Control	July 7, 1995	1.0

4.9 Process Control

Briefly describe how all processes are controlled to ensure that only correct and acceptable items are produced and used in fabrication. Also describe how processes involving special/critical characteristics (due to government safety and environmental regulations, fit, function, or appearance) are monitored and controlled. Also describe the responsibilities and authority of the individuals/functions involved in process control.

4.9.1 Process Monitoring and Operator Instructions

Briefly describe how processes are monitored, process set-ups are verified, and appearance items are checked. Refer to related documented procedures and work instructions for all employees having responsibility for operation of processes.

4.9.2 Preliminary Process Capability Requirements

Briefly describe how process capabilities are determined and verified. Refer to the Production Part Approval Process Manual and continuous improvement techniques while preparing process capability studies.

4.9.3 Ongoing Process Performance Requirements

Briefly describe how ongoing process performance requirements such as Cpk and Ppk are determined and monitored.

Approved by:	Issued by:
Signature:	Signature:
Approval Date:	Issue Date:
Revision:	Revision Date:

Logo	**QUALITY ASSURANCE MANUAL**	Page of

SECTION	SUBJECT	EFFECTIVE DATE	REVISION
4.9	Process Control (contd)	July 7, 1995	1.0

4.9.4 Modified Preliminary or Ongoing Capability Requirements

If the company modifies some of its process performance requirements, show them in the control plan.

4.9.5 Verification of Job Set-Ups

Briefly describe how job set-ups are verified so that producing parts meet all requirements. Prepare documented process set-up instructions for set-up technicians. If applicable, use statistical verification techniques and last-off part comparison.

4.9.6 Process Changes

Describe the production part approval process from the customer when any changes occur in engineering drawing, manufacturing location, material sources, or the production process environment.

4.9.7 Appearance Items

Briefly describe how "appearance items" designated by customers are manufactured. In particular, describe verification areas and the qualifications and experience of verification personnel.

Approved by:	Issued by:
Signature:	Signature:
Approval Date:	Issue Date:
Revision:	Revision Date:

Logo	**QUALITY ASSURANCE MANUAL**	Page of

SECTION	SUBJECT	EFFECTIVE DATE	REVISION
4.10	Inspection and Testing	July 7, 1995	1.0

4.10.1 General

Briefly describe how all inspection and testing activities are planned and executed in order to verify and assure conformance of an item or activity to specific requirements. Also describe the responsibilities and authority of all verification personnel.

4.10.2 Receiving Inspection and Testing

Briefly describe the incoming inspection process for verification of conformance to specified requirements in accordance with the quality plan (control plan) and refer to the documented procedures.

4.10.3 In-Process Inspection and Testing

Briefly describe the in-process inspection and testing of products as required by the quality plan (control plan) and refer to the documented procedures.

4.10.4 Final Inspection and Testing

Briefly describe the final inspection and testing process in accordance with the quality plan (control plan) and refer to the documented procedures.

4.10.5 Inspection and Test Records

Briefly describe how records of inspection and test records are maintained. These records must show clearly whether the product has passed or failed inspections according to defined acceptance criteria. Records should identify the inspection authority responsible for the release of the product.

Approved by:	Issued by:
Signature:	Signature:
Approval Date:	Issue Date:
Revision:	Revision Date:

Logo	**QUALITY ASSURANCE MANUAL**	Page of

SECTION	SUBJECT	EFFECTIVE DATE	REVISION
4.11	Control of Inspection, Measuring, & Test Equipment	July 7, 1995	1.0

4.11.1 General

Briefly describe how inspection, measuring, and test instruments (including test software) are controlled, calibrated, and maintained to demonstrate conformance of the product to the specified requirements. Also describe the responsibilities and authority of the individuals/functions involved in these activities.

4.11.2 Control Procedure

Briefly describe the process used for calibration of inspection, measuring, and test equipment, including details of equipment types, identification, location, frequency of checking, checking method, acceptance criteria, and action to be taken when results are unsatisfactory.

4.11.3 Inspection, Measuring, and Test Equipment Records

Briefly describe how records of calibration/verification activities on all inspection, measuring, and test equipment are maintained, how equipment failures are logged, and how repairs of failures are recorded. Also explain how the customer is informed if suspect materials are shipped by mistake.

4.11.4 Measurement Systems Analysis

Briefly describe how appropriate statistical studies are conducted to analyze the variation present in inspection, measuring, and test equipment. Follow the analytical methods and acceptance criteria provided in Measurement Systems Analysis Reference Manual.

Approved by:	Issued by:
Signature:	Signature:
Approval Date:	Issue Date:
Revision:	Revision Date:

Logo	**QUALITY ASSURANCE MANUAL**		Page of
SECTION	*SUBJECT*	*EFFECTIVE DATE*	*REVISION*
4.12	Inspection and Test Status	July 7, 1995	1.0

4.12 Inspection and Test Status

Describe how inspection and test status of all products are recorded and maintained as defined in the quality plan (control plan). Also describe the responsibilities and authority of the individuals/functions involved in the activities described in this section.

Example

Procedures have been developed for identifying the operation and inspection status of products. The status of inspection and test activities of all manufactured products is identified at all times throughout the manufacturing process. Their status is maintained through the use of manufacturing operation status sheets (traveler sheets). These travelers become part of the final documentation. Thus, the inspection and test status of all components is indicated on the work-in process (WIP) travel card. As each inspection and test activity is completed, the inspector circles the appropriate result and initials the card.

Upon receipt, incoming material is routed to the inspection area. After inspection, the inspection status of the material is indicated by travelers and routing labels which accompany the material.

Approved by:	**Issued by:**
Signature:	**Signature:**
Approval Date:	**Issue Date:**
Revision:	**Revision Date:**

Logo	**QUALITY ASSURANCE MANUAL**	Page of

SECTION	SUBJECT	EFFECTIVE DATE	REVISION
4.13	Control of Nonconforming Product	July 7, 1995	1.0

4.13.1 General

Briefly describe how nonconforming products are identified, segregated, evaluated, recorded, and disposed of.

Example

Nonconforming materials, parts, or products which are purchased or manufactured in-house are promptly identified, segregated, and controlled. Responsible individuals are promptly contacted to determine disposition. Repaired or reworked items are re-examined in accordance with applicable procedures, and all actions taken are documented.

4.13.2 Review and Disposition of Nonconforming Product

Briefly describe the responsibilities and authority of the functions/ individuals involved in review and disposition of nonconforming product.

4.13.3 Control of Reworked Product

Briefly describe the rework policy and procedures and ensure that they are accessible and utilized by appropriate personnel in their work areas.

4.13.4 Engineering-Approved Product Authorization

Briefly describe the responsibilities and authority of the functions/ individuals involved in review and disposition of nonconforming product.

Approved by:	Issued by:
Signature:	Signature:
Approval Date:	Issue Date:
Revision:	Revision Date:

Logo	**QUALITY ASSURANCE MANUAL**	Page of

SECTION	SUBJECT	EFFECTIVE DATE	REVISION
4.14	Corrective and Preventive Action	July 7, 1995	1.0

4.14.1 General

Briefly describe the corrective action plan, showing how corrective and preventive actions are taken and who is responsible for taking these actions. Also describe individual authority and responsibilities. All corrective or preventive action plans should attempt to eliminate the cause of the actual or potential nonconformity.

Example

The corrective and preventive action process has been implemented in a defined and structured manner throughout the organization. It is an ongoing activity. Actions are taken as a result of data collected and analyzed to control and improve processes and quality of support components. Input to this process includes analysis of nonconforming materials, evaluation of suppliers' performance, in-process control, inspection and test data, delivery performance and shipment integrity, mean time to failure data, customer feedback, and results from internal audits.

The quality department is responsible for monitoring the corrective action process, including ensuring that all process and procedural changes made as a result of corrective actions are documented. Responsibility for monitoring the effectiveness of the changes is shared by the quality department and the process owners of the relevant department(s).

Approved by:	Issued by:
Signature:	Signature:
Approval Date:	Issue Date:
Revision:	Revision Date:

Logo	**QUALITY ASSURANCE MANUAL**		Page of
SECTION	*SUBJECT*	*EFFECTIVE DATE*	*REVISION*
4.14	Corrective and Preventive Action (contd)	July 7, 1995	1.0

4.14.2 Corrective Action

Briefly describe how customer complaints and reports of product non-conformity are handled effectively, their causes investigated, corrective actions determined, and control applied for prevention.

4.14.3 Preventive Action

Briefly describe how information from appropriate sources, such as processes and work operations which affect product quality, quality records, audit results, and customer complaints, are analyzed and used to prevent potential occurrence of defects.

Approved by:	Issued by:
Signature:	Signature:
Approval Date:	Issue Date:
Revision:	Revision Date:

Logo	**QUALITY ASSURANCE MANUAL**	Page of

SECTION	*SUBJECT*	*EFFECTIVE DATE*	*REVISION*
4.15	Handling, Storage, Packaging, Preservation, and Delivery	July 7, 1995	1.0

4.15.1 General

Briefly describe how quality is maintained in handling, storage, packaging, preservation, and delivery of products. Also describe responsibilities and authority of functions/individuals involved in these activities.

Example

Incoming material is stored after verification by the receiving department and, if specified, incoming inspection that the components are as expected. Requests for outgoing material can only be generated by authorized personnel. The processes for both storage and pulling of material are documented. Receipt into and pulling from stores is documented and recorded systematically.

4.15.2 Handling

Briefly describe how handling of product is carried out in order to prevent damage and deterioration.

4.15.3 Storage

Briefly describe how designated storage areas are used and managed in order to prevent damage and deterioration of products before their use or delivery. Also describe the appropriate method of receipt and issue of products from storage areas.

Approved by:	Issued by:
Signature:	Signature:
Approval Date:	Issue Date:
Revision:	Revision Date:

Logo	**QUALITY ASSURANCE MANUAL**		Page of
SECTION	*SUBJECT*	*EFFECTIVE DATE*	*REVISION*
4.15	Handling, Storage, Packaging, Preservation, and Delivery (contd)	July 7, 1995	1.0

4.15.4 Packaging

Briefly describe how all materials to be shipped are properly packaged and labeled according to customer requirements. Refer to Customer Packaging Standard.

4.15.5 Preservation

Briefly describe the appropriate methods for preservation and segregation of products for safekeeping as long they are under the control of the company.

4.15.6 Delivery

Briefly describe the delivery policy and procedures in order to achieve the highest level of delivery performance. Also describe how delivery problem information is communicated to the customer.

Example

Delivery approval and monitoring of carriers are the responsibility of the traffic group. The selection criteria for carriers include reviewing their ability to ensure that product quality will be protected and preserved during transport to the final destination as well as on-time delivery performance. Shipment integrity metrics are in place to monitor these requirements.

Approved by:	Issued by:
Signature:	Signature:
Approval Date:	Issue Date:
Revision:	Revision Date:

Logo	**QUALITY ASSURANCE MANUAL**		Page of
SECTION	*SUBJECT*	*EFFECTIVE DATE*	*REVISION*
4.16	Control of Quality Records	July 7, 1995	1.0

4.16 Control of Quality Records

Briefly describe how information about the quality system is identified, collected, retained, retrieved, and updated. Also describe the responsibilities and authority of the individuals/functions involved in activities mentioned in this section. Records may be retained in any form of media such as hard copy or electronic. Refer to QS-9000 Element 4.16 for length of time various records must be retained.

Example

A large volume of information is regularly created within the quality system. It is retained within the division in the form of paper records, microfiche, and computer files. Records are identified by the batch, component, or process as applicable, securely stored, and retrieved as necessary. These records and reports cover a number of activities, including new product introduction, engineering changes, nonconforming material reports, inspection records, mean time to failure data, equipment calibration and maintenance records, internal quality audit results, supplier performance evaluations, shipment details, repair/manufacturing support plans, and management reviews of the quality system.

Each department within the division is responsible for safe storage and retrieval of records in its own area. Overall responsibility for monitoring the retention process resides with the controller of records.

All records are maintained for a minimum of three months. Critical records are retained for a minimum of three years.

Approved by:	Issued by:
Signature:	Signature:
Approval Date:	Issue Date:
Revision:	Revision Date:

Logo	**QUALITY ASSURANCE MANUAL**	Page of

SECTION	SUBJECT	EFFECTIVE DATE	REVISION
4.17	Internal Quality Audits	July 7, 1995	1.0

4.17 Internal Quality Audits

Briefly describe how the internal quality audit function carries out its activities to assure that the quality assurance system has been operating effectively. Also describe the authority and responsibilities of the individuals/functions involved in internal quality audits. Results of all audit activities must be recorded and brought to the attention of the personnel responsible for the activities being audited. Refer to ISO 10011 as a guide to quality system audits.

Example

The internal quality audit program consists of program audits, external audits, and special audits performed on a scheduled basis. Unannounced random internal audits are conducted at least once a year by trained personnel from the quality assurance department. Each individual member of the audit team is a certified ISO 9000 quality auditor.

The internal audit team follows accepted audit practices (see reference). Records of all audits, including nonconformities and corrective actions taken, are maintained by the quality managers. A copy of all such audits is distributed to all individuals included on the quality manual distribution list.

Approved by:	Issued by:
Signature:	Signature:
Approval Date:	Issue Date:
Revision:	Revision Date:

Logo	**QUALITY ASSURANCE MANUAL**	Page of

SECTION	SUBJECT	EFFECTIVE DATE	REVISION
4.18	Training	July 7, 1995	1.0

4.18 Training

Briefly describe how all levels of employees are trained so that they can carry out their duties effectively. Also describe the responsibilities and authority of the individuals/functions involved in training activities at all levels. Also maintain appropriate records of all training activities.

Example

A comprehensive training program which ensures that all levels of employees can carry out their duties effectively has been developed and carried out for all levels of staff. It covers areas such as personal development, technical know-how, safety, on-the-job training, total quality control (TQC) methodologies, and other needed disciplines. The training is provided by specialists. For example, TQC classes are offered by trained experts in the quality department, engineering specifications and design (ESD) training is given by the division's ESD engineer, etc.

Each supervisor is responsible for training each employee who reports to him or her. Each department maintains a matrix for each employee. This matrix lists the courses taken by the employee. Each employee also maintains a personal development plan as part of the yearly evaluation process. The development plan includes action to be taken to maintain or enhance the employee's skills. The development plans are reviewed yearly. A copy of each employee's development plan is kept in his or her personnel file.

Approved by:	Issued by:
Signature:	Signature:
Approval Date:	Issue Date:
Revision:	Revision Date:

Logo	**QUALITY ASSURANCE MANUAL**		Page of
SECTION	*SUBJECT*	*EFFECTIVE DATE*	*REVISION*
4.18	Training (contd)	July 7, 1995	1.0

4.18 Training (continued)

Each employee has an individual job plan. This job plan is matched to a job description which defines the skill level and qualifications necessary for the job. Employees are selected based upon their ability to meet the job requirements specified in the job description. Copies of all job descriptions are maintained by the personnel department.

To ensure that new employees have a full understanding of the standards of operation, an organizational model was developed and communicated in writing to all supervisors. This model includes actions such as training classes, on-the-job training, mentoring, and more.

Based upon job responsibilities, classes are also offered, and certification showing successful completion of training is required before an employee can assume the job responsibility. Certification records are maintained in the relevant departments, with copies kept in the employees' files.

Approved by:	Issued by:
Signature:	Signature:
Approval Date:	Issue Date:
Revision:	Revision Date:

Logo	QUALITY ASSURANCE MANUAL		Page of
SECTION	SUBJECT	EFFECTIVE DATE	REVISION
4.19	Servicing	July 7, 1995	1.0

4.19 Servicing

This section must be included where servicing is a specific require-ment. Briefly describe how servicing of products is performed, verified, and reported to meet specified customer requirements.

Approved by:	Issued by:
Signature:	Signature:
Approval Date:	Issue Date:
Revision:	Revision Date:

Logo	**QUALITY ASSURANCE MANUAL**		Page of
SECTION	*SUBJECT*	*EFFECTIVE DATE*	*REVISION*
4.20	Statistical Techniques	July 7, 1995	1.0

4.20.1 Identification of Need

Briefly describe how the need for various statistical methods is identified to establish, control, and verify process capability and product characteristics. Also describe how these methods are implemented in the analysis of quality-related data at all levels of the organization. Describe the responsibilities and authority of the individuals/functions involved in using statistical analysis of quality-related data.

Example

Statistical methods have been used extensively throughout the organization to analyze quality-related data, present information, and develop forecasts and trends. Techniques commonly used include statistical sampling, statistical process control, quality function deployment, fishbone diagram, Pareto analysis, Taguchi methods, design of experiment, regression and correlation analysis, exponential smoothing techniques, and time series analysis.

Approved by:	Issued by:
Signature:	Signature:
Approval Date:	Issue Date:
Revision:	Revision Date:

Logo	**QUALITY ASSURANCE MANUAL**		Page of
SECTION	*SUBJECT*	*EFFECTIVE DATE*	*REVISION*
4.20	Statistical Techniques (contd)	July 7, 1995	1.0

4.20.2 Procedures

Briefly describe how application of statistical techniques is implemented. Refer to Fundamental Statistical Process Control Reference Manual in this respect.

Example

For marketing analysis, customer surveys are carried out on a yearly basis. Results from these surveys are analyzed to determine the level of customer satisfaction, as well as opportunities for future products and services. The following areas are regularly monitored by statistical techniques: materials, vendor qualification, delivery performance, shipment audits, process control, and departmental and divisional quality performance.

Approved by:	Issued by:
Signature:	Signature:
Approval Date:	Issue Date:
Revision:	Revision Date:

Logo	**QUALITY ASSURANCE MANUAL**	Page of

SECTION	SUBJECT	EFFECTIVE DATE	REVISION
5.1	Production Part Approval Process	July 7, 1995	1.0

5.1.1 General

Briefly describe the purpose and scope of the production part approval process (PPAP) and the responsibilities and authority of the functions/individuals involved in this process. Production part approval is granted for a part number, engineering change level, manufacturing location, production process environment, and material subcontractor. Refer to the PPAP Manual.

Example

Product part review and approval is submitted for each part prior to the first quality shipment and for engineering change level, manufacturing location, material subcontractor(s), and production process environment. If there are any changes in these items, customers are immediately notified and the PPAP resubmitted. Directions provided in the *PPAP Manual* published by the AIAG and prescribed formats are closely followed in preparing and submitting the required documentation to the appropriate authority of the customer for review and approval

5.1.2 Engineering Change Validation

Briefly describe how validation of all engineering changes is verified. Refer to the PPAP Manual in this respect.

Approved by:	Issued by:
Signature:	Signature:
Approval Date:	Issue Date:
Revision:	Revision Date:

Logo	**QUALITY ASSURANCE MANUAL**		Page of
SECTION	*SUBJECT*	*EFFECTIVE DATE*	*REVISION*
5.2	Continuous Improvement	July 7, 1995	1.0

5.2.1 General

Briefly describe how the company is engaged in continuous improvement of quality and productivity. Describe the action plans for continuous improvement of processes and implementation of quality and productivity improvement projects related to machine downtime, die set-up and machine changeover times, scrap, rework, repair, waste of labor and materials, nonvalue-added floor space and times, excessive handling and storage costs, customer complaints, excessive variation from target, difficult assembly of products, etc.

5.2.2 Quality and Productivity Improvements

Briefly describe how opportunities for quality and productivity improvement are identified and appropriate improvement projects are implemented.

5.2.3 Techniques for Continuous Improvement

Demonstrate knowledge and use of analytical techniques such as design of experiments, theory of constraints, value analysis, problem solving, benchmarking, control charts, capability indices, cumulative sum charting, etc. in preparing the action plans. Refer to the action plans here and document them separately. Also describe the responsibilities and authority of the individuals/functions involved in the above-mentioned continuous improvement activities.

Approved by:	**Issued by:**
Signature:	**Signature:**
Approval Date:	**Issue Date:**
Revision:	**Revision Date:**

Logo	**QUALITY ASSURANCE MANUAL**	Page of

SECTION	SUBJECT	EFFECTIVE DATE	REVISION
5.3	Manufacturing Capabilities	July 7, 1995	1.0

5.3.1 Facilities, Equipment, Process Planning, and Effectiveness

Briefly describe the facility plans, process plans, and equipment plans in conjunction with the Advanced Quality Planning (AQP) process. You may refer to the AQP document for these plans. Use cross-functional teams and mistake-proofing in developing these plans.

5.3.2 Mistake-Proofing

Briefly describe failure mode and effects analysis, capability studies, and service reports. Also describe how mistake-proofing methodology is used in planning processes, facilities, equipment, and tooling and in resolving problems.

5.3.3 Tool Design and Fabrication

Briefly describe how tool and gage design, fabrication, and full dimensional inspection are carried out using appropriate technical resources. Also describe the system that maintains the list of tool and gage suppliers approved by customers, tracks and follows up on subcontractors, and keeps track of customer-owned tools and dies.

5.3.4 Tooling Management

Describe the tooling management system for maintenance, repair, storage, retrieval, and set-up of tools, dies, fixtures, and perishable tools. These documents must be mentioned here even if they are maintained at a different location. Also describe the responsibilities and authority of the individuals/functions involved in activities associated with this section.

Approved by:	Issued by:
Signature:	Signature:
Approval Date:	Issue Date:
Revision:	Revision Date:

APPENDIX B

FORMAT FOR A QUALITY ASSURANCE PROCEDURE

There are various ways to write a quality assurance procedure. Because a registrar may prefer a particular format, checking with the registrar before starting to write a procedure may save a lot of time. A typical and commonly used format includes six distinct paragraphs, as follows:

1.0 **Purpose:** Why was this procedure written?

2.0 **Scope:** Which activities are covered by this procedure?

3.0 **Definitions:** Definition of any unknown terms

4.0 **References:** Listing of documents referred to in this procedure

5.0 **Procedure:** Step-by-step description of the procedure

6.0 **Records and forms:** Listing of any form or recording document

A quality assurance procedure can be easily explained with a flowchart. A flowchart is prepared by drawing a number of blocks and connecting them with lines and arrows to show the step-by-step procedure. Blocks of different shapes are used when drawing a flowchart. A rectangle is used to represent an operation, a diamond is used for a decision, and a triangle is used to indicate holding or storage.

A sample quality assurance procedure with a flowchart is presented here as an example. Most quality assurance procedures can be written using this example as a model. A suggested format for the table of contents of a quality assurance procedure manual is also included.

NAME OF THE COMPANY

Location of the Plant
Address & Telephone No.

QUALITY ASSURANCE PROCEDURES

Control Copy No.

Developed and Issued By

Date of Initial Issue

Approved by
Date of Approval

Revision No.
Date of Revision

Logo	**QUALITY ASSURANCE PROCEDURE**		Page of
SECTION	*SUBJECT*	*EFFECTIVE DATE*	*REVISION*
1001	Table of Contents	July 5, 1995	1.0

The following is a typical format for the table of contents page of a quality assurance procedure.

Table of Contents

Number	*Subject*	*Effective Date*	*Revision*
1001	Table of contents	July 5, 1995	1.0
1002	Document control	July 5, 1995	1.0
1003	Design control	July 5, 1995	1.0
1004	Procurement document control	July 5, 1995	1.0
1005	Receiving inspection	July 5, 1995	1.0
1006	Handling, storage, and distribution	July 5, 1995	1.0
1007	Control of nonconforming materials	July 5, 1995	1.0
1008	In-process inspection	July 5, 1995	1.0
1009	Final inspection and testing	July 5, 1995	1.0
1010	Measuring and test equipment	July 5, 1995	1.0
1011	Test and operating status	July 5, 1995	1.0
1012	Special processes	July 5, 1995	1.0
1013	Packaging and shipping	July 5, 1995	1.0
1014	Corrective action	July 5, 1995	1.0
1015	Internal audit	July 5, 1995	1.0

Approved by:	**Issued by:**
Signature:	**Signature:**
Approval Date:	**Issue Date:**
Revision:	**Revision Date:**

Logo	**QUALITY ASSURANCE PROCEDURE**	Page of

SECTION	SUBJECT	EFFECTIVE DATE	REVISION
1002	Document Control	July 5, 1995	1.0

This is a suggested format for a sample quality assurance procedure entitled Document Control.

Document Control

1.0 PURPOSE

    1.1 To assure that all drawings and documents are correctly prepared, readily available, and properly controlled

2.0 SCOPE

    2.1 Includes all drawings and documents prepared and in use

3.0 DEFINITIONS

    3.1 None

4.0 REFERENCES

    4.1 Design control procedure

5.0 PROCEDURE

    5.1 *Design engineer* assigns a drawing number to the engineering drawing and records the drawing number, title of the drawing, initials of the person preparing the drawing, and date of issue

    5.2 *Design engineer* reviews the drawing using the proper design control procedure

    5.3 *Design engineer* approves the drawing or returns the drawing for correction to the person who originally prepared it

Approved by:	**Issued by:**
Signature:	**Signature:**
Approval Date:	**Issue Date:**
Revision:	**Revision Date:**

Logo	**QUALITY ASSURANCE PROCEDURE**	Page	of

SECTION	*SUBJECT*	*EFFECTIVE DATE*	*REVISION*
1002	Document Control (contd)	July 5, 1995	1.0

Document Control (continued)

5.4   *Design engineer* forwards the approved drawing to the print room, with his or her approval signature and date of approval

5.5   *Print room operator* files drawings by drawing number in sequential order

5.6   *Print room operator* microfilms all drawings that are six or more months old.

5.7   *Requester* fills out *print request form* to request prints

5.8   *Print room operator* copies original drawings per request

5.9   *Print room operator* stamps all copies with date of issue and forwards them to the requester

5.10 *Design engineer* requests original tracing by filling out *out card*

5.11 *Print room operator* removes original drawing from file, places the out card in the file, and forwards the original to design engineer

5.12 *Design engineer* sends original to the *draftsperson* who originally prepared the drawing for revision

Approved by:	Issued by:
Signature:	Signature:
Approval Date:	Issue Date:
Revision:	Revision Date:

Logo	**QUALITY ASSURANCE PROCEDURE**		Page of
SECTION	*SUBJECT*	*EFFECTIVE DATE*	*REVISION*
1002	Document Control (contd)	July 5, 1995	1.0

Document Control (continued)

5.13 *Draftsperson* revises the drawing using proper procedures and assigns a revision number to the revised drawing

5.14 *Design engineer* reviews the revision and approves it with signature and date

5.15 *Design engineer* informs all departments affected by the change and returns original to print room for filing

6.0 RECORDS AND FORMS

   6.1 *Out card*

   6.2 *Print request form*

Approved by:	Issued by:
Signature:	Signature:
Approval Date:	Issue Date:
Revision:	Revision Date:

Logo	**QUALITY ASSURANCE PROCEDURE**		Page of
SECTION	*SUBJECT*	*EFFECTIVE DATE*	*REVISION*
1002	Document Control (contd)	July 5, 1995	1.0

The following is a suggested format for a flowchart of the document control procedure.

Flowchart of Document Control Procedure

5.1	Assign a drawing #	5.10	Request for original	5.7	Request for print
5.2	Review drawings	5.11	Remove original	5.8	Copy original
5.3	Approve drawings	5.12	Send original for revision	5.9	Stamp copies and issue them
5.4	Send drawings to print room	5.13	Revise original		
5.5	File original	5.14	Approve revision of original		
5.6	Microfilm old ones	5.15	Notify affected functions and return original		

Approved by:	**Issued by:**
Signature:	**Signature:**
Approval Date:	**Issue Date:**
Revision:	**Revision Date:**

APPENDIX C

GLOSSARY OF TERMS

Accreditation: The authorization an organization receives from an accrediting body to conduct quality system assessments and registrations/certifications.

Accreditation mark: An insignia that indicates accreditation. Only accrediting bodies and the companies accredited by them are allowed to use an accreditation mark.

Accrediting body: An organization that authorizes other organizations to conduct quality system assessments and registrations/certifications of supplier companies.

Assessment: The process by which a registrar determines compliance to standards (or lack thereof) on the part of a supplier company. The assessment involves meetings between the registrar's representatives/auditors and the supplier company's representatives, on-site visits to closely audit the supplier company's operations, a report by the auditors to their registration board, and a final decision to grant or deny certification to the supplier company.

Audit: A planned, documented, and independent assessment of a quality system to determine whether the system meets the agreed upon requirements.

Audit program: The documented program for planning and performing quality audits.

Auditee: An organization being audited.

Auditor: A person qualified and authorized to perform audits.

Certification: The "seal of approval" a supplier company receives when it has implemented the requirements of a specific standard, has been audited by a registrar, and has been found to be in complete compliance with the standard. Such companies are then given certificates of approval that state with which standards they are in compliance and that feature the marks of the registrar and the registrar's accrediting body.

Certifying body: A quality systems registration organization (registrar) that has been accredited to assess supplier companies' quality systems and grant them certificates stating that they are in full compliance with a particular standard (for example, ISO 9001, ANSI/ASQC 991, EN 29001, etc.).

Compliance: An affirmative indication that the company meets the agreed upon requirements.

Conformity assessment activities: Those activities that involve the examination or auditing of operations to determine conformity/compliance to a given standard or other specific requirements.

Contractor: The company that provides products or services to its customers under a contractual agreement.

Contractual standards: Standards written in very precise language with direct phrases which tell the implementers of the standards exactly what they must do. These standards try to make very clear what is required, and they are meant to be included in the appendix of a contract. ISO 9001, 9002, and 9003 are all examples of contractual standards.

Co-registration agreement: An understanding between two (or more) registrars that one will recognize the audits/assessments conducted by the other. When registrar A has determined that a supplier company is in full conformance with a specific standard and decides to grant that supplier a certificate of registration, registrar B will generally accept registrar A's audit results without conducting its own audit. (The supplier company may have to pay an additional fee to receive a second certificate of approval from registrar B.) There must be a high level of trust between organizations that enter into co-registration agreements with each other.

Corrective action: Action taken to eliminate the cause of an existing nonconformity.

Customer: Consumer, user, client, beneficiary, or second party.

Design review: A formal, documented, systematic, and comprehensive examination of design activities in order to determine compliance with design requirements and to identify problems for possible corrective actions.

Finding: A conclusion made based upon observations.

First party: In terms of quality system standards, the first party is the company that is implementing (and seeking full conformance with) the provisions of a particular standard. When standards are written in first-party mode, the supplier seeks to assess itself against (and bring its own systems into conformance with) the provisions of the standard.

Follow-up audit: Audit performed to verify that corrective action is carried out.

Guideline standards: Standards that are meant to provide the managers of organizations with guidance on how to build or improve their quality systems. ISO 9004 is an example of a guideline standard.

Inspection: Decision to accept or reject a product based upon observation from measurement and testing of one or more characteristics of a product or service and comparing it with specified standards or requirements.

Internal audit: An audit conducted by a supplier company to assess its own operation, look for areas of nonconformance (to the ISO 9000 standard or other standard against which it is assessing itself), and uncover any other quality problems or inconsistencies that could impair the quality of its products or services.

Mark of certification/registrar mark: A special logo used by quality system registrars. Each registrar has its own mark design. When a supplier company has been assessed by a registrar and has achieved certification, the registrar's mark appears on the supplier's certificate, along with the mark of the organization that has accredited the registrar. These marks can then be used on the certified company's advertising literature, letterhead, business cards, etc. However, the registrar's marks may not be used on products or on product packaging, as the registrar has only certified the supplier company's quality system and not its products.

Mutual recognition: An agreement among conformity assessment organizations of various countries to accept the results of one another's conformity assessment activities. (As of this writing, there is no international system for mutual recognition, although many countries are attempting to work toward this goal.)

Nonconformity: The nonfulfillment of a specified requirement.

Nonregulated/unregulated products: Products that do not fall into any of the categories of regulated products. For nonregulated products, there is no directive in place by the European Community and they do not require the CE mark (see Appendix G). However, many customers still require that their suppliers of nonregulated products conform to particular standards, including ISO 9000.

Notified body: An organization that has been authorized by a European Community member state's government or recognized accrediting body to conduct conformity assessment activities.

Organization: A company, corporation, enterprise, firm, or association that has its own administration and functions.

Organizational structure: The formal delegation of authority and responsibilities and the coordinational relationship through which an organization works.

Pre-assessment: A visit by a registrar to a supplier company to discuss and gauge the company's readiness for assessment and registration to the appropriate quality system standard.

Preliminary evaluation: A mock audit conducted by registrars to assess a supplier company's readiness for a final registration audit.

Procedure: A specified way to perform an activity.

Process: A set of interrelated activities which transform inputs into desired outputs.

Product: The desired output from a process.

Product directive: A mandatory rule issued by European Community legislation which prescribes a level of safety and performance that twenty-three (as of this writing) categories of products must meet.

The purpose of the legislated product directives is to protect European consumers of these products. Of these twenty-three categories, fourteen reference ISO-9000-based factory control systems (under the title EN 29000) as a means of meeting government requirements. For each of these products, there is a date by which suppliers must comply with the acceptable standards/requirements.

Product quality audit: Assessment of conformance to required product characteristics.

Purchaser: The customer in a contractual situation.

Quality: The total features and characteristics of a product or service that bear on its ability to satisfy stated or implied needs of the customer.

Quality assurance: All planned and systematic activities involved in demonstrating and providing sufficient confidence that the system will meet the specified quality requirements.

Quality control: The operational techniques and activities involved in implementing quality.

Quality management: All management activities including quality policy, organization structure, quality planning, quality control, quality assurance, and continuous improvement of the quality system.

Quality manual: The document that describes the quality policy and the quality system of a company.

Quality plan: A documented process of setting out the specific quality practices, resources, and activities for achieving quality objectives related to a particular product or contractual requirements.

Quality planning: All activities involving the preparation of a quality plan.

Quality policy: The overall objectives of and directions from top management relating to quality.

Quality surveillance: The continuous monitoring and verification of the status of the quality system with reference to the stated requirements.

Quality system: The structure, procedures, processes, and resources needed to implement the quality system requirements.

Registration: The act by a quality systems registrar of granting a certificate of approval to a supplier company that has been found to be in full compliance with a specific quality system standard.

Second party: When referring to quality system standards, this is the customer of the supplier company. For second-party standards, the customer ascertains the quality conformance of the supplier. (*see* First party)

Subcontractor: A company that provides a product or service to the supplier.

Supplier: An organization that provides a product or service to the customer.

Survey: A collection of desired information and examination of that information for some specific purpose.

Testing: A way to determine whether an item meets specific requirements by subjecting it to a set of physical, chemical, and operating actions and conditions.

Third party: When referring to quality system standards, the third party is the registration organization that assesses the supplier company's (first party's) quality system for conformance to a particular standard.

Total quality management: A management approach to quality for achieving customer satisfaction through participation of all the members and functions of the organization.

Traceability: The ability to trace an item or entity using identification of records.

Validation: The process of evaluating software to determine its compliance with specific requirements.

Verification: The process involving review, testing, checking, auditing, and inspection to determine and document whether a quality system complies with the specified requirements.

APPENDIX D

QUALITY SYSTEM REGISTRARS

The following is a list of quality system registrars that offer registration services for the ISO 9000 series of quality management and assurance standards. Those marked with two asterisks (**) are also QS-9000 qualified, making them eligible to conduct audits on the QS-9000 quality system requirements. This information was provided in *AIAG 1995 Quality Survey*, published by AIAG, Southfield, Michigan, and confirmed by ANSI/RAB on September 15, 1995. The list is subject to additions or deletions at any time, as new registrars start up or existing ones cease operations. Similarly, a current ISO 9000 registrar may become QS-9000 qualified and extend its services to QS-9000 registration. Note that this list is provided for informational purposes only and is not intended to be an endorsement of any particular organization's services. To obtain a current list of registrars, contact the accreditation bodies.

REGISTRARS LOCATED IN THE UNITED STATES

ABS Quality Evaluations, Inc.**
American Bureau of Shipping
16855 Northchase Drive
Houston, TX 77060-6008
Phone: 713-873-9400, Fax: 713-874-9564

AIB-Vincotte (AV Qualite)
2900 Wilcrest, Suite 300
Houston, TX 77042
Phone: 713-465-2850, Fax: 713-465-1182

American Association for Laboratory Accreditation
656 Quince Orchard Road, #304
Gaithersburg, MD 20878-1495
Phone: 301-670-1377, Fax: 301-869-1495

American European Services, Inc.
1054 31st Street, NW, Suite 120
Washington, DC 20007
Phone: 202-337-3214, Fax: 202-377-3709

American Gas Association Quality**
A Division of American Gas Association Laboratories
8501 East Pleasant Valley Road
Cleveland, OH 44131
Phone: 216-524-4990, Fax: 216-642-3463

American Quality Assessors
1201 Main Street, Suite 2010
Columbia, SC 29202
Phone: 803-254-1164, Fax: 803-252-0056

American Society of Mechanical Engineers, The
United Engineering Center
345 E 47th Street
New York, NY 10017
Phone: 212-605-4796, Fax: 212-605-8713

AT&T Quality Registrar
650 Liberty Avenue
Union, NJ 07083
Phone: 800-521-3399, Fax: 908-851-3360

Bellcore Quality Registration
6 Corporate Place, Room 1A230
Piscataway, NJ 08854
Phone: 908-699-3739, Fax: 908-336-2244

Bureau Veritas Quality International (NA), Inc.**
North American Central Offices
509 North Main Street
Jamestown, NY 14701
Phone: 716-484-9002, Fax: 716-484-9003

Det Norske Veritas Certification, Inc.**
16340 Park Ten Place, Suite 100
Houston, TX 77084
Phone: 713-579-9003, Fax: 713-579-1360

DLS Quality Technology Associates, Inc.
108 Hallmore Drive
Camillus, NY 13031
Phone: 315-468-5811, Fax: 315-699-6332

Electronic Industries Quality Registry
2001 Pennsylvania Avenue NW
Washington, DC 20006-1813
Phone: 202-457-4970, Fax: 202-457-4985

Entela, Inc., Quality Systems Registrar**
3033 Madison Avenue SE
Grand Rapids, MI 49548
Phone: 616-247-0515, Fax: 616-247-7527

ETL Testing Laboratories
Industrial Park
Cortland, NY 13045
Phone: 502-ISO-9000 or 607-753-6711

Factory Mutual Research Corporation
1151 Boston-Providence Turnpike
P.O. Box 9102
Norwood, MA 02062
Phone: 617-255-4883, Fax: 617-762-9375

Intertek Services Corporation**
9900 Main Street, Suite 500
Fairfax, VA 22031-3969
Phone: 703-476-9000, Fax: 703-273-4124

KEMA Registered Quality Incorporated
4379 County Line Road
Chalfont, PA 18914
Phone: 215-822-4281, Fax: 215-822-4271

KPMG Quality Registrar**
150 West Jefferson, Suite 1200
Detroit, MI 48226-4497
Phone: 313-983-0344, Fax: 313-983-0500

Lloyd's Register Quality Assurance Ltd.**
c/o Lloyd's Register Shipping
33-41 Newark Street
Hoboken, NJ 07030
Phone: 201-963-1111, Fax: 201-963-3299

MET Laboratories Incorporated
914 W. Patapsco Avenue
Baltimore, MD 21230
Phone: 410-354-3300, Fax: 410-354-3313

National Quality Assurance, Ltd.
1146 Massachusetts Avenue
Boxborough, MA 01719
Phone: 508-635-9256, Fax: 508-266-1073

National Standards Authority of Ireland
North American Certification Services
5 Medallion Center (Greeley Street)
Merrimack, NH 03054
Phone: 603-424-7070, Fax: 603-429-1427

OMNEX-Automotive Quality Systems Registrar, Inc.**
P.O. Box 15019
Ann Arbor, MI 48106
Phone: 313-480-9940, Fax: 313-480-9941

OTS Quality Registrars, Inc.
10700 Northwest Freeway, Suite 455
Houston, TX 77092
Phone: 713-688-9494, Fax: 713-688-9590

Quality Assurance Association of France
Woodfield Executive Center
1101 Perimeter Drive, Suite 450
Schaumburg, IL 60173
Phone: 708-330-6006, Fax 708-330-0707

Quality System Registrars, Inc.**
13873 Park Center Road, Suite 217
Herndon, VA 22071-3279
Phone: 703-478-0241, Fax: 703-478-0645

Scott Quality Systems Registrar, Inc.
8 Grove Street, Suite 200
Wellesley, MA 02181
Phone: 617-239-1110, Fax: 418-646-3315

SGS International Certification Services, Inc.**
Meadows Office Complex
301 Route 17 North
Rutherford, NJ 07070
Phone: 201-935-1500, Fax: 201-935-4555

Smithers Quality Assessments, Inc.**
425 W. Market Street
Akron, OH 44303-2099
Phone: 216-762-4231, Fax: 216-762-7447

Steel Related Industries Quality System Registrars**
2000 Corporate Drive, Suite 300
Wexford, PA 15090
Phone: 412-934-9000, Fax: 412-935-6825

TRA Certification
700 E. Beardsley Avenue
P.O. Box 1081
Elkhart, IN 46515
Phone: 219-264-0745, Fax: 219-264-0740

Tri-Tech Services, Inc.
4700 Clairton Boulevard
Pittsburgh, PA 15236
Phone: 412-884-2290, Fax: 412-884-2768

TUV America
5 Cherry Hill Drive
Danvers, MA 01923
Phone: 508-777-7999

TUV Essen**
1032 Elwell Court, Suite 222
Palo Alto, CA 94303
Phone: 415-961-0521, Fax: 415-961-9119

TUV Rheinland of North America, Inc.**
12 Commerce Road
Newtown, CT 06470
Phone: 203-426-0888, Fax: 203-426-3156

Underwriters Laboratories Inc.**
333 Pfingsten Road
Northbrook, IL 60062-2096
Phone: 708-272-8800, Fax: 708-272-8129
1285 Walt Whitman Road
Melville, NY 11747-3081
Phone: 516-271-6200, Fax: 516-271-6242

REGISTRARS LOCATED IN EUROPE AND CANADA

Association Espanola de Normalizacion y Certificacion (AENOR)
(Spanish Association for Standardization and Certification)
Fernandez de la Hoz, 52
28010 Madrid, Spain
Phone: 34 1 410 4851

Association Francaise pour l'Assurance de la Qualite (AFAQ)
(French Association for Quality Assurance)
Tour Septentrion Cedex 9
F92081 Paris la Defense, France
Phone: +33 (1) 47 73 49 49, Fax: +33 (1) 47 73 49 99
Telex: AFAQ 6200307 F

British Standards Institution Quality Assurance (BSI)**
Quality Assurance Centre Linford Wood
P.O. Box 375
Milton Keynes
Buckinghamshire MK 14 GLE United Kingdom
Phone: +44-90-822-0908, Fax: +44-90-822-0671

Canadian General Standards Board
(Office) 9C 1 Phase 3
Place du Portage
11 Laurier Street
Hull, Quebec
(Mail) Qualification and Certification Listing Branch CGSB
222 Queen Street, Suite 1402
Ottawa, Ontario K1A 1G6, Canada
Phone: 613-941-8657, Fax: 613-941-8706

Ceramic Industry Certification Scheme, Ltd.
Queens Road, Penkhull
Stoke-On-Trent, ST4 7LQ United Kingdom
Phone: +44-782-411-008, Fax: +44-782-412-331

CGA Approvals
55 Scarsdale Road
Toronto, Ontario M3B 2R3, Canada
Phone: 416-447-6468, Fax: 416-447-7067

GBJD Registrars Ltd.
22 Clarissa Drive, Suite 822
Richmond Hill, Ontario L4C 9R6, Canada
Phone: 905-508-9417, Fax: 905-471-0822

**German Association for the Certification of Quality
Management Systems**
August-Schanz Str. 21
D-60433 Frankfurt/Main, Germany
Phone: 49-69-954213-0, Fax: 49-69-954213-11

Litton Systems Canada Ltd.
Quality System Registrars
25 City View Drive
Etobicoke, Ontario M9W 5A7, Canada
Phone: 416-249-1231 Ext. 2308 or 800-267-0861, Fax: 416-246-2049

Loss Prevention Certification Board, Ltd., The
Melrose Avenue
Borehamwood, Hertfordshire WD6 2BJ
United Kingdom
Phone: 44-081-207-2345, Fax: 44-081-207-6305

Quality Certification Bureau, Inc.
#208, Advanced Technology Center
9650 - 20th Avenue
Edmonton, Alberta T6N 1G1, Canada
Phone: 800-268-7371, Fax: 403-496-2464

Quality Management Institute (QMI)**
A division of the Canadian Standards Association
Suite 800, Mississauga Executive Center
Two Robert Speck Parkway
Mississauga, Ontario L4Z 1H8, Canada
Phone: 905-272-3920, Fax: 905-272-3942

Quebec Quality Certification Group
70, Rue Dalhousie, Bureau 220
Quebec, Quebec G1K 4B2, Canada
Phone: 418-643-5813, Fax: 418-646-3315

SGS International Certification Services Canada, Inc.
90 Gough Road, Unit 4
Markham, Ontario L3R 5V5, Canada
Phone: 905-479-1160, Fax: 905-479-9452

Sira Certification Service
Sira Test and Certification Ltd.
Saighton Lane
Saighton, Chester CH36EG
United Kingdom
Phone: 44-024-433-2200, Fax: 44-024-433-2112

Underwriters Laboratories of Canada**
7 Crouse Road
Scarborough, Ontario M1R 3A9, Canada
Phone: 416-757-3611, Fax: 416-757-1781

Warnock Hersey Professional Services, Ltd.
8810 Elmslie Street
LaSalle, Quebec H8R 1V8, Canada
Phone: 514-366-3100, Fax: 514-366-5350

APPENDIX E

ACCREDITING BODIES

The following is a list of ISO accrediting bodies in various countries. These accrediting bodies can direct you toward registrars that would be appropriate for your company's particular markets in the United States and the European Community.

BELGIUM

Belgium's National Accreditation Council for Quality Systems
Ministere des Affaires Economiques
Administration de l'Industrie
Square de Meeus, 23
B-1040 Brussels, Belgium

For additional information, contact:

IBN
Avenue de la Brabanconne, 29
B-1040 Brussels, Belgium
Phone: 02 734 92 05, Fax: 02 734 42 64, Telex: 23 877 Benor

Note: For Belgium, AIB Vincotte is the EQNET member.

DENMARK

The National Agency of Industry and Trade
Tagensvej 137
2200 Copenhagen N Denmark
Phone: +31 85 10 66, Fax: +31 81 70 68, Telex: 15768 indtra dk

Note: The QA Certification Department of the Danish Standards Association (DS) has been accredited by the Dutch accreditation body, Raad voor de Certiflcatie (RvC) and by the National Agency of Industry and Trade. DS is the EQNET member.

FRANCE

Association Francaise pour l'Assurance de la Qualite (AFAQ)
(French Association for Quality Assurance)
Tour Septentrion Cedex 9
F92081 Paris la Defense, France
Phone: +33 (1) 47 73 49 49, Fax: +33 (1) 47 73 49 99,
Telex: AFAQ 6200307 F

AFAQ has a number of accredited registrars listed by field; the competence of these registrars to certify companies to ISO 9000 standards has been demonstrated. AFAQ is the EQNET member for France. AFAQ has mutual recognition agreements with DQS (German certifying body/registrar), SQS (Swiss certifying body/registrar), and QMI (Canadian certifying body/registrar). AFAQ can also be contacted through American European Services, Inc. (AES).

GERMANY

Traegergemeinschaft fuer Akkreditierung GmbH (TAG)
Gustav-Heinemann-Ufer 84-88
5000 Koln 51 Germany
Phone: +49 (221) 3 70 86 37, Fax: +49 (221) 3 70 87 30

TAG is the German accreditation body for all certifiers/registrars. The German Accreditation Council, Deutschen Akkreditierungs Rat (DAR) handles QSR (Quality System Registrar) approvals. Deutsche Gesellschaft zur Zertiiizierung von Qualitatssicherungs systemen mbH (DQS) is an accredited registrar. DQS is the EQNET member.

IRELAND

National Standards Association of Ireland (NSAI)
Certification Division
Glasnevin
Dublin - 9 Ireland
Phone: +353 1 37 0101, Fax: +353 1 36 9821

NSAI operates under the Irish Science and Technology Agency. NSAI is the EQNET member.

ITALY

Sistema Nazionale de Certiflcazione (SINCERT)
Via Battistotti Sassi, 11
I-20123 Milano, Italy
Phone: 01139 2 700241, Fax: 01139 2 70106106

The Italian accreditation/certification system is represented by SINCERT. There are several registrars in Italy; CISQ is the EQNET member.

NETHERLANDS

Raad voor de Certificatie (RvC)
Dutch Council for Accreditation
Stationsweg 13 F
3972 KA Driebergen, Netherlands
Phone: +03438 12604, Fax: +03438 18554

RvC is the only European accrediting body that accredits registrars outside its country. NV Kema, a quality system registrar, is the EQNET member for the Netherlands.

NORWAY

Norsk Akkreditering Direktoratet for Maleteknikk
(Directorate of the National Service of Legal Metrology)
P.O. Box 6832 St. Olavs Place
N-0130 Oslo, Norway
Phone: +47 2 20 02 40, Fax: +47 2 20 77 72

The Norwegian Certification System (NCS) is the EQNET member for Norway.

SPAIN

Associacion Espanola de Nonnalizacion y Certificacion (AENOR)
(Spanish Association for Standardization and Certification)
Fernandez de la Hoz, 52
28010 Madrid, Spain
Phone: 34 1 410-4851

The Spanish accreditation/certification system is represented by AENOR.

SWEDEN

Standardiseringskommissionen i Sverige (SIS)
Box 3295
10366 Stockholm, Sweden
Phone: +46 8 613 52 00, Fax: +46 8 11 70 35

Swedish registrars include Det Norske Veritas and Lloyd's Register. SIS is the EQNET member for Sweden.

UNITED KINGDOM

National Accreditation Council for Certifying Bodies (NACCB)
3 Birdcage Walk
London SWlH 9JH UK
Phone: 01 222 5374, Fax: 01 222 0197, Telex: 9413487 UK SERV G

NACCB-approved registrars include the British Standards Institution (BSI), Quality Assurance Centre, Linford Wood, Milton Keynes, Buckinghamshire MK14 GLE, UK (phone: +44 908 220908, fax: +44 908 220671). BSI is the EQNET member for the United Kingdom.

UNITED STATES

Registrar Accreditation Board (RAB)
American Society for Quality Control (ASQC)
611 East Wisconsin Avenue
Milwaukee, Wl 53202
Phone: 414-272-8575, Fax: 414-272-1734

APPENDIX F

SOURCES OF INFORMATION FOR THE EC MARKET

The following is a list of pertinent phone numbers and addresses for information on the EC Internal Market Program, copies of the Single Internal Market regulations, background information on the European Community, or assistance regarding specific opportunities or potential problems pertaining to your company's particular product area.

Single Internal Market information service

Office of European Community Affairs
U.S. Department of Commerce
Room 3036
14th and Constitution Avenue, NW
Washington, DC 20230
Phone: 202-377-5276, for standards information: 202-377-5279

For information on trade development, consult the following:

Textiles and apparel
U.S. Department of Commerce
Office of Textiles and Apparel, Room 3109
Washington, DC 20230
Phone: 202-377-2043

Service industries
U.S. Department of Commerce
Office of Service Industries, Room 1124
Washington, DC 20230
Phone: 202-377-3575

Chemicals, construction industry products, and basic industries
U.S. Department of Commerce
Office of Basic Industries, Room 4043 or 4045
Washington, DC 20230
Phone: 202-377-0614

Information technology, instrumentation, and electronics
U.S. Department of Commerce
Office of Telecommunications, Room 100 1A
Washington, DC 20230
Phone: 202-377-4466

Autos and consumer goods
U.S. Department of Commerce
Office of Automotive Affairs and Consumer Goods, Room 4324
Washington, DC 20230
Phone: 202-377-2762

Construction projects and industrial machinery
U.S. Department of Commerce
Office of the DAS for Capital Goods and International
  Construction, Room 4045
Washington, DC 20230
Phone: 202-377-0614

Aerospace
U.S. Department of Commerce
Office of Aerospace, HC HB, Room 2130
Washington, DC 20230
Phone: 202-377-2835

For advice or information about any aspect of exporting to the EC, contact your International Trade Administration (ITA) district office or speak to an ITA European country desk officer:

Belgium, Luxembourg
202-377-5401

Greece
202-377-3945

Portugal
202-377-3945

Denmark
202-377-3254

Ireland
202-377-2177

Spain
202-377-4508

France
202-377-8008

Italy
202-377-2177

United Kingdom
202-377-3748

Germany
202-377-2434

Netherlands
202-377-5401

Brochures, official documents, and studies on the EC's internal market programs are available on request from the EC delegation, which can be reached by calling:

The Delegation of the Commission of the European Communities
Office of Press and Public Affairs
Public Inquiries Section
Washington, DC 20230
Phone: 202-862-9500 (10 a.m. to 4 p.m. Monday through Thursday)

The National Institute of Standards and Technology (NIST) has prepared an extensive summary of EC initiatives on standards and other related material. This information can be obtained by contacting:

GATT (General Agreement on Tariffs and Trade)
Inquiry Point/Technical Office
Office of Standards Code and Information
National Institute of Standards and Technology
Building 411, Room A163
Gaithersburg, MD 20899
Phone: 301-975-4040
GATT hotline: 301-975-4041

The National Center of Standards and Certification Information (NCSCI)
National Institute of Standards and Technology
Building 411, Room A163
Gaithersburg, MD 20899
Phone: 301-975-4040

Additional U.S. government contacts are:

U.S. Department of State
Europe/Regional, Political and Economic Affairs
Room 6519
Washington, DC 20520
Phone: 202-647-2395

DAUSTR (Deputy Assistant United States Trade Representative
for Europe and the Mediterranean)
600 17th Street, NW
Washington, DC 20506
Phone: 202-395-3320

APPENDIX G

ACRONYMS

AIAG (Automotive Industry Action Group): The organization that disseminates automotive-industry-related information. AIAG has published many major QS-9000-related documents, including *Quality System Requirements: QS-9000, Measurement Systems Analysis Manual, Advanced Product Quality Planning Manual, Statistical Process Control Manual, Production Part Approval Process Manual,* and *Quality System Assessment Manual.*

ANSI (American National Standards Institute): Ensures that its member organizations empowered to write standards follow rules of consensus and broad participation by interested parties. ANSI is the U.S. member to the International Organization for Standardization (ISO).

ASQC (American Society for Quality Control): A technical society made up of quality professionals. ASQC has over 100,000 members throughout the world, but the majority are from the United States. ASQC publishes quality-related American National Standards, including the ANSI/ASQC Q90 series, the U.S. version of ISO 9000. ASQC is the sole owner of the Registrar Accreditation Board (RAB).

BSI (British Standards Institute): The United Kingdom's standards-writing body.

BSIQA (British Standards Institution Quality Assurance): An accredited certification body (registrar) in the United Kingdom, with branches in Canada and the United States.

CASE (Conformity Assessment Systems Evaluation): A proposal under which the U.S. Department of Commerce would guarantee U.S. conformity assessment operations. The proposal includes how all those schemes would actually be guaranteed by the Department of Commerce. It describes three basic levels of conformity assessment: (1) the conformity level, at which certification and registration organizations assess the conformance to standards of products and systems; (2) the accreditation level, at which certification and registration organizations are formally accredited; and (3) the recognition level, at which the accreditation agencies are formally recognized.

CE Mark (Conformite European [European Conformity] Mark): This mark on a product indicates that the product has been manufactured under a factory product control/quality system that conforms to mandatory European primary safety requirements. For twenty-three product categories for which there are European directives, the CE Mark must appear on a product before that product can be exported to the European Community. The CE Mark must also appear on any European product covered by the directive before it can be sold in a store. Companies can obtain the CE mark for fourteen of the twenty-three categories of regulated products through a factory product control system (EN 29000) that is based on ISO 9000.

CEN (European Committee for Standardization): Publishes regional standards (for EC and EFTA) covering nonelectrical/nonelectronic subject fields.

DIN (Deutsches Institut fur Normung): Germany's standards-writing body.

DIS (Draft International Standard): DIS standards are international standards that are still in draft form and are being reviewed for publication.

EAC (European Committee for Accreditation of Certification Bodies): An organization whose members represent the accreditation organizations of all EC and EFTA member states. It appears that it aspires to be designated as a specialized committee for accreditation in the EOTC. Its mission will likely be to harmonize rules for accreditation, to facilitate mutual recognition of accreditation, and to provide advice and counsel to other committees in the EOTC framework on matters related to accreditation.

EC (European Community): A framework within which member states have agreed to integrate their economies and eventually form a political union. Currently, there are twelve members: Belgium, Denmark, France, Germany, Greece, Ireland, Italy, Luxembourg, Netherlands, Portugal, Spain, and the United Kingdom.

EEC (European Economic Community): Comprised of EC and EFTA countries.

EFQM (European Federation for Quality Management): A European organization of upper-level managers concerned with quality.

EFTA (European Free Trade Association): A framework within which its members strive to remove import duties, quotas, and other obstacles to trade and to uphold liberal, nondiscriminatory practices in world trade. Current members are Austria, Finland, Iceland, Norway, Sweden, Switzerland, and Liechtenstein.

EN 45000: A series of standards developed by the EC to regulate and harmonize certification and accreditation activities.

EOQ (European Organization for Quality): An independent organization whose mission is to improve quality and reliability of goods and services primarily through publications, conferences, and seminars. Members are quality-related organizations from countries throughout Europe, including Eastern-bloc countries. ASQC is an affiliate society member.

EOTC (European Organization for Testing and Certification): Set up by the EC and EFTA to focus on conformity assessment issues in regulated spheres. Its purpose is to facilitate the development of certification systems and mutual recognition agreements.

EQNET (European Network for Quality System Assessment and Certification): A business arrangement among quality system certification bodies (registrars). Its mission is to simplify the process for obtaining quality system certificates in the several countries in which a multinational supplier operates. The member registrars issue several certificates simultaneously after performing a joint audit.

EQS (European Committee for Quality System Assessment and Certification): Formed with the expectation that it will be designated as the specialized committee for quality systems in the EOTC. Its members are individual experts or delegations, not organizations.

Members are appointed by each EC and EFTA country. The function of the EQS is to harmonize rules for quality system assessment and certification (registration) to facilitate mutual recognition of registrations and to provide advice and counsel to other committees in the EOTC framework on matters related to quality system assessment and certification.

ETL (ETL Testing Laboratories): A U.S. product testing and certification organization that has entered the quality system registration field.

EUROLAB (European Organization for Laboratory Testing): Formed with the expectation that it will be designated as the specialized committee for testing in the EOTC. The function of EUROLAB is to provide an interface between the testing community and other concerned parties, to accelerate development and harmonization of test methods, to promote mutual acceptance of test results, and to provide to the EOTC expertise in the field of testing.

GATT (General Agreement on Tariffs and Trade): An international agreement signed in 1948 for the purpose of facilitating trade, decreasing trade barriers, reducing tariffs, and avoiding protectionism.

IEC (International Electrotechnical Commission): A worldwide organization that produces standards in the electrical and electronic fields. Members are national committees composed of representatives of the various organizations that deal with electrical/electronic standardization in each country. IEC was formed in 1906.

IQA (Institute of Quality Assurance): A British organization for quality professionals. It operates a widely recognized system of certification for auditors of quality systems.

ISO (International Organization for Standardization): Formed in 1947, ISO is a worldwide federation of some ninety national standards bodies. It promotes the development of standardization and related activities to facilitate the international exchange of goods and services. It also develops intellectual, scientific, technological, and economic cooperation among member countries. ISO has a number of technical committees, subcommittees, working groups, and ad hoc study groups. All these groups represent the manufacturers, suppliers, users, engineers, testing laboratories, public services, governments, consumer groups, and research organizations of each of the member countries.

LRQA (Lloyd's Register for Quality Assurance): Founded in 1760 in London, England, for the purpose of inspecting and classifying marine vessels. In 1985, LRQA was formed as a subsidiary of Lloyd's Register of Shipping to provide independent third-party quality system registration. LRQA was accredited by the NACCB in 1986. In 1986 it was also accredited for quality management system certification by the Dutch government under the program administered by the RvC.

MOU (Memorandum of Understanding): A mutually agreed upon written document among a number of organizations covering specific activities of common interest. EQS was established with a MOU, as was EQNET. There are a number of MOU agreements covering mutual recognition of quality system registration in which one of the signatories is a non-European registrar. Under such agreements, an additional certificate can be acquired from the European registrar (for an additional fee in many cases) which will then be recognized in Europe.

NACCB (National Accreditation Council for Certification Bodies): Formed in 1984, NACCB is the British authority for accreditation of third-party registrars of quality systems.

NIST (National Institute of Standards and Technology): An agency of the U.S. Department of Commerce. It is headquartered in Gaithersburg, Maryland. NIST has been involved with accrediting testing laboratories for several years. It has not yet become directly involved with accrediting assessors of quality systems such as the ISO 9000 series.

QMI (Quality Management Institute): The Canadian registrar of quality systems. It is a part of the Canadian Standards Association (CSA).

QMI (Quality Management International): A British consultancy in the field of quality.

RAB (Registrar Accreditation Board): A subsidiary of ASQC, RAB is a U.S. organization whose dual mission is to recognize the competence and reliability of registrars of quality systems and to achieve international recognition of the registrations issued by RAB-accredited registrars. The RAB also certifies quality system auditors.

RvC (Raad voor de Certificatie [Council for Certification for the Netherlands]): Formed in 1980, RvC is the Dutch authority for recognizing the competence and reliability of organizations that perform third-party certification of products, accreditation of laboratories, and/ or registration of quality systems.

TAG (Technical Advisory Group): A group composed of experts who represent U.S. business and industry. These groups are responsible for building consensus, helping to form U.S. positions on important standardization issues, and encouraging U.S. experts to participate in international working groups.

TC (Technical Committee): A committee formed by the International Organization for Standardization. These committees are composed of international experts from business and industry. Their purpose is to develop and build consensus on various types of standards. ISO TC 176 (Quality Management and Quality Assurance) is one such Technical Committee. It was formed in 1979, and its first published set of standards (in 1987) was the ISO 9000 series.

UL (Underwriters Laboratories): A U.S. product testing and certification organization. It is also a quality system registrar. UL conducts ISO 9000 assessments under several co-registration agreements with various international organizations.

Appendix H

CASE STUDY: THE ISO 9001 ROAD TO QS-9000 AND BEYOND

John H. Leaning

Manager, Quality Systems, Detroit Diesel Corporation

Detroit, Michigan

ABSTRACT

Detroit Diesel Corporation (DDC) achieved ISO 9001 registration in January 1994. This was the first planned step toward QS-9000 registration. Detroit Diesel Corporation's product lines and markets served, size of the organization and facilities, and reasons for implementing ISO 9001 are outlined here. Established quality systems credentials are described, which provides a baseline from which ISO 9001 was developed. The planning and progress made by utilization of the quality steering committee, internal and external audits, and lead assessor training are also described. The very

John H. Leaning was actually involved in the creation of QS-9000 through the truck advisory group.

important issue of management support and a wide variety of vital communication tools that were employed are covered in detail. Employee awareness and involvement in the total process through training and performing self-audits together with participation in ISO quizzes were key factors in developing "Team DDC" success. Finally the "Lessons Learned" throughout the implementation process, third-party audit, and subsequent periodic audits are identified.

CONTENTS OF THE CASE

1. Scope of Product Lines and Markets Served
2. Brief History and Facilities Profile
3. Established Quality System Credentials
4. Reasons for Implementing ISO 9001
5. The Preparation and Warm-Up Lap
6. The First Assessment Lap
7. Follow-Up Strategy Developed
   - ISO Awareness—Training Needs Unfold
   - Internal Auditing Plan
   - Communication Developments
   - Team Spirit and Motivation
   - Top Management—Support
8. Follow-Up Audit Lap
9. Lessons Learned
10. Subsequent Laps

SCOPE OF PRODUCT LINES AND MARKET SERVED: GENERAL

Detroit Diesel Corporation is a leading U.S. manufacturer of heavy-duty diesel engines. With V.M. Motori joining the company in January 1995, Detroit Diesel is now a team of 6,300 employees engaged in the design, manufacture, sales, and service of heavy-duty diesel, alternative fuel engines, automotive diesel engines, and engine parts around the world. This complete line of more than 500 engine models ranges from 5 to 10,000 horsepower, including collaborative marketing arrangements.

Detroit Diesel's customers are found around the world in the truck, coach and bus, automobile, construction, mining, marine, industrial, power generation, and military markets. The company serves its customers and markets through its manufacturing plants in Redford, Michigan and Cento, Italy; an assembly operation in Kansas; four re-manufacturing centers strategically located throughout the United States; three parts distribution centers worldwide; and an international distribution and support network of 118 authorized distributors and 2,300 dealers.

BRIEF HISTORY

- Roots can be traced back to 1938 with the formation of the Detroit Diesel Engine Division by General Motors. The primary product was the series 71 engine, which was extensively used in World War II.

- In 1970, General Motors consolidated its Detroit Diesel Division and Allison Division in Indianapolis to form Detroit Diesel–Allison Division.

- On January 1, 1988, a joint venture was formed between Penske Corporation and General Motors, and Detroit Diesel Corporation became the successor to the heavy-duty diesel engine business.

- In October 1993, the initial public offering of common stock was made.

FACILITIES PROFILE

Redford, Michigan

- Size: 3.0+ million square feet

- Employees: 3500 (approximately 2200 represented by the UAW)

Canton PDC, Ohio

- Size: 575,000 square feet
- Employees: 270 approximately

Redford Facility Products

Two cycle engines ranging from 75 to 2,925 horsepower

- Series 53; I-3, I-4, V6
- Series 71; I-3, I-4, I-6, V6, V8, V12, V16
- Series 92; 6V, 8V, 12V, 16V
- Series 149; 8V, 12V, 16V, 20V

Four cycle engines ranging from 250 to 500 horsepower

- Series 50; I-4
- Series 60; I-6

ESTABLISHED QUALITY SYSTEM CREDENTIALS

Military and Type Approvals

- U.S. government military specifications
  - Quality system; Mil-I-45208A
  - Calibration system; Mil-Std-45662A

Type Approvals

- American Bureau of Shipping
- Det. Norske Veritas
- Lloyd's Register of Shipping
- Korean Register of Shipping

Quality Program Awards

- U.S. Army Contractor Performance Certification Program (CP)^2
- Ford Motor Company "Q1 Preferred Quality Award"
- Freightliner Corporation "Masters of Quality" Supplier Award
- Pierce "Quality Achievement Supplier" Award for Outstanding Performance
- Oshkosh Truck "Certified Supplier" Award
- Sullair "Certificate of Achievement" Supplier Award

REASONS FOR IMPLEMENTING ISO 9001

DDC wanted to develop a cultural change:

- Allow for and encourage innovation
- Assure ongoing product consistency
- Drive for continuous improvement
- Provide for transfer of critical knowledge
- Provide a road map of how to do things right and get them done quickly
- Allow for a more streamlined organization, minimizing duplication of effort
- Allow greater emphasis to focus on the needs of the customer and reduce costs which are quality related
- Quality system design that has breadth and depth
- Support the quality mission statement

ISO 9001 PROVIDED THE MODEL/MEANS TO ACHIEVE DDC'S QUALITY STRATEGY GOALS

Quality Mission Statement

DDC's quality mission statement is as follows:

> To provide a quality product that satisfies our customers' needs and expectations the first time every time.

> Our goal is to satisfy our customer needs whether it be through timely delivery; providing the best value for the money; efficient and courteous service; or superior quality, reliability, and durability of our products. As such, we have committed ourselves to the following:

1. Understanding and responding to our customers' needs and expectations

2. Providing "proven design" products

3. Improving the system of production to generate continuing quality and productivity improvements

4. Developing a highly-trained and motivated work force with full accountability and responsibility

5. Establishing long-term relations with suppliers

6. Continual improving on all of the above

Additional Reasons for Implementing ISO 9001

- Customers indicating potential future expectations:
  - Truck OEMs
  - U.S. government

- Participation in development of future common quality standard (QS-9000)

- Marine classification societies quality system requirements were becoming aligned with ISO 9000

- Registration had potential of reducing the number of quality system audits by marine and OEM customers

THE PREPARATION AND WARM-UP LAP

- Recognized value of established quality system credentials
- October 1991 Lloyd's Register of Shipping System Survey, ISO 9001 based
- Established the Corporate Quality Steering Committee in July 1992
- Selected registrar and established date for assessment
- Completed system development of tier 1 document (second tier existed)
- Walk and talk around facility with consultant December 1992
- Consultant provided customized training of ISO 9001 overview sessions to over 170 managers, support engineers, and auditors
- Registrar conducted brief planning visit to each facility and completed document—review report January 1993

THE FIRST ASSESSMENT LAP

- Registrar's audit team comprised:
  - Redford   20 man-days
  - Canton   4 man-days
- DDC was impressed with audit team's experience and professionalism
- The RvC matrix scoring system was selected by DDC
- All corrective action requests (CARs) were viewed positively as opportunities for improvement
- Audit results summary (initial)
  - Documentation degree of conformity 100%
  - Degree of implementation—71% versus 75% minimum
  - Eight elements did not meet requirements

FOLLOW-UP STRATEGY DEVELOPED

- Explain what was needed to address CARs and assign functional leaders and/or small teams
- Develop ISO training needs
- Utilize ongoing internal audits to identify more "opportunities"
- Develop communication methods
- Develop team spirit and motivation
- Assure ongoing top management support

ISO Awareness—Training Needs Unfold

A. Strengthening of quality system auditing
  - Three attended lead auditor training (March/April)

B. Investigate previous ISO 9000 success stories
  - Dow Corning Corp. visit (April)

C. Quality mission statement understood
  - Video produced by President of DDC (June)

D. To prepare everyone
  - Employee ISO overview sessions (September)
  - Developed by salary/hourly team
  - 2700 attended
  - 45 minutes + Q&A
  - Handout material provided
  - Video made for absentees and external operations

E. ISO familiarization to develop "self-checking" capabilities (November)
  - Employee programs developed for managers, supervisors, and engineers
  - "Non-Conformances" video produced with help from contract auditor
  - "Check Lists" developed
  - ISO eyeballs calibrated

Internal Auditing Plan

- Try to maintain the established audit schedule by hiring supplementary help if needed

- Continue to look for compliance concerns and system improvement opportunities

- Try to close out both third-party and new internal systems CARs prior to follow-up audit by registrar

- Sweep audit and "frown faces"—after team readiness feedback

Communication Developments

- Business update meetings by CEO and COO covered ISO expectations

- Employee overview sessions, topics included:
  - ISO 9000 standards
  - Developments in the U.S.
  - Status of competition
  - Benefits of registration
  - What to expect from the registrar
  - What is expected from DDC
  - Conduct during audit
  - How to help team Detroit Diesel achieve certification
  - Handout package

- Update letters published, which included:
  - Progress made
  - Areas requiring focus
  - Helpful reminders
  - Countdown

- ISO quizzes
  - Informative by design
  - Wacky humor injected
  - $100 value prizes

- Countdown boards
  - Three weeks prior to audit
  - Daily count

Team Spirit and Motivation

- Constructive assistance to everyone
- Provide ISO awareness training
- Encourage "self-checking" activities
- Recognize accomplishments
- Keep the team informed
- Encourage supervisors and groups to work together on ISO solutions
- Use a little humor
- Quizzes to encourage ISO 9001 discussion
- Sense of urgency supported
- Reinforce continuous improvement as ongoing theme

Top Management—Support

- Monthly, then weekly quality steering committee meetings
  - Progress reported
  - Barriers identified
  - Resource needs discussed
- Provided with examples of benefits realized
- Ongoing monitoring of expressed doubts or concerns
  - Responses were provided
- Requested in critical situations to become personally involved

FOLLOW-UP AUDIT LAP

- Audit results summary (final)
  - Documentation degree of conformity 100%
  - Degree of implementation—94% vs. 75% minimum
  - All elements met requirements
- The checkered flag...
  - But no finishing line

LESSONS LEARNED (FROM THE ISO 9001 REGISTRATION PROCESS)

- Top-level management commitment is vital
- Communication needs should not be underestimated
- Team involvement is critical for ownership and pride
- "Say what you do"—the value in documenting it
- "Do what you say"—discipline is mandated
- ISO 9001—tool for improvement
- Internal systems audits—training and support are critical

"EFFORT EQUALS RESULTS"*

SUBSEQUENT LAPS

- First periodic audit—successful
- Second periodic audit—upgrade achieved to ISO 9001, 1994 rev.
- QS-9000 system refinements presently being implemented
- QS-9000 pre-assessment
- QS-9000 assessment
- QS-9000 registration
- Ongoing compliance and continually improving per the Detroit Diesel Corporation quality mission statement

---

*DDC's motto.

INDEX